# West Virginia
## The Illegal State

Jeremy T.K. Farley

FEATURING THE WORK OF James c. McGregor, Ph.D.
### *The Disruption of Virginia*
Published in 1922

## FRONT COVER PHOTOS
### Boy Miner
A young trapper boy inside Turkey Knob Mine in West Virginia.

### Stonewall Jackson
"Chancellorsville" portrait, taken seven days before the general was fatally
wounded during the Battle of Chancellorsville.

### Three Young Miners
Photo of coal miners in West Virginia in 1908

### Two Young Miners
Photo of child miners in 1908

### Statue of Abraham Lincoln
"Abraham Lincoln Walks at Midnight" Statue on the grounds of the West Virginia
State Capitol.  Photo credit: "Snoopywv"

To my late great-grandfather, Thomas Benton Farley.
A man who embodied what it means to be a Mountaineer.

# FEATURING THE WORK OF
# JAMES C. MCGREGOR, PH.D.
# "THE DISRUPTION OF VIRGINIA"

In 1922, JAMES c. McGregor, Ph.D., published a 328-page book entitled, *The Disruption of Virginia*. In his publication, McGregor shared interviews with hundreds of West Virginians who had lived through the Civil War – pouring his life into researching dusty documents detailing the creation of West Virginia, the scholarly historian reached the conclusion that the West Virginia Statehood Act was both blatantly unconstitutional and never desired by any more than a small minority of the people of the mountains.

In the 93 years since its publication, *The Disruption of Virginia* has become a forgotten relic of history – lost to generations of West Virginians.

Today, McGregor's words, research and points are more important than ever before, serving as a significant foundation for the understanding of West Virginia's statehood and turbulent history.

**West Virginia: The Illegal State** is a modern adaption of McGregor's work, featuring extensive portions of *The Disruption of Virginia* to the reader – edited and transformed into modern day language and complimented by the words of coalfield historian Jeremy T.K. Farley.

Jeremy is a native of Mingo County, West Virginia, and great-great-great grandson of Thomas B. Farley, a lifelong resident of Logan County and valiant defender of Virginia during the War Between the States.

Championing the cause of Southern West Virginia, Jeremy lays out a case asserting that much of the Mountain State's disproportionate level of poverty – especially in the southern region – can be directly attributed to the illegal creation of West Virginia and the subsequent neglect following the West Virginia Statehood Act – America's coup d'état.

# CONTENTS

| | Note to the Reader | 7 |
|---|---|---|
| I. | A Tale of Two Virginias | 11 |
| II. | Early Seeds of Disunion & Union | 25 |
| III. | The Election of Abraham Lincoln | 39 |
| IV. | Virginia's Path to War | 53 |
| V. | The First Wheeling Convention | 65 |
| VI. | The Second Wheeling Convention | 81 |
| VII. | West Virginia's Corrupt Root | 97 |
| VIII. | Carving Up the Map | 117 |
| IX. | The Civil War in Western Virginia | 133 |
| X. | West Virginia's First Constitution | 149 |
| XI. | West Virginia Goes to Congress | 171 |
| XII. | Becoming the 35th Star | 185 |
| XIII. | An Illegal State of Chaos | 201 |

## Contact the Author:

Send an email:     publisher@appalachianmagazine.com

Twitter:     @JeremyTKFarley

Facebook:     Facebook.com/AuthorJeremyFarley

# A NOTE TO THE READER

In the years leading up to the American Revolutionary War, my 6x great-grandfather, Thomas Buery Farley, the descendant of early English settlers from eastern Virginia, moved his family westward, crossing the Shenandoah Valley and entering the mountains of Western Virginia.

Starting a farm along the banks of the New River, in what would later become Giles County, my ancestor would eventually grow old and succumb to the fate that awaits all men.

Like so many others from his era, he too would be buried on his farm beneath a sandstone grave, marking the final resting place of one of the tens of thousands of men who sacrificed their blood and sweat in order to birth a nation dedicated to preserving the common rights of men – a nation "for the people and by the people."

Though his headstone has since become unreadable, his legacy in this part of the nation is still remembered.

A monument in honor of his contribution to the settling of Virginia's western mountains quietly overlooks a tributary of the New River, just a handful of miles south of Pearisburg, at a park named Farley Wayside.

PHOTO: This is a photo of me at the Thomas Farley Memorial Monument located at Farley Wayside Park in Giles County, Virginia.

His descendants continued where he left off, pushing farther north and west into the interior of the Kanawha Valley. There, they served as one of the region's early salt producers.

Ultimately, my ancestors would settle along the banks of the Tug Fork of the Big Sandy River in what was for many years, Logan County, Virginia.

At the outbreak of the American Civil War, my great-grandfather's grandfather, Thomas Benton Farley, did the very same thing his great-grandfather had done nearly a century earlier – took up arms in defense of his homeland, Virginia.

Though the state and county he called home have changed names in the century and a half that followed that terrible war, the place my family has called home has not. Burch, Logan County, Virginia, is now Delbarton, Mingo County, West Virginia, the product of decades of political mistrust and a never ending game of tug-of-war played out in courtrooms and legislative halls.

Though the county seat has changed and the state flag is now a different color, the parcel of ground all fifteen of my great-great-great grandfather's children were born upon has remained virtually unchanged.

Still in the Farley name, the land stands as a silent testimony of our family's rich and proud heritage. For us, home is not about the seat of state government or the color of a flag, but instead, it is the story of us. The story of a mountain people who have both commanded the respect and fear of anyone wishing to cross them or their jagged borders.

Dating back to the days my ancestors first crossed into this intrepid territory, life has been cruel; they knew this from the moment they mounted the top of the Blue Ridge and made the fateful decision to press onward, in fact, the challenge of survival is the very thing that drove them to the mountains in the first place.

They never made it rich in Appalachia, but that was never their goal. For them, the tranquil isolation offered by the mountains was reward enough.

Sadly, the impenetrable walls surrounding them were not enough to shield their communities from powerful industrialists who lived in faraway cities – word of unimaginable riches both blanketing the mountains (timber) and blanketed by the mountains (coal) traveled quickly to centers of commerce around the globe.

The greed of outside tyrants has, on several occasions, forced the people who call this region home to take up arms and wage wars against ruling elitists from distant lands – tyrants whose sole desire was to exploit the people and their abundantly rich lands.

Still yet, the individuals who call West Virginia home have remained resilient. They have met each new challenge with an unmatched zeal and passion.

*Montani Semper Libri*, Mountaineers are Always Free.

I am a Mountaineer and in this book, I will seek to share the true story of how the Mountain State was formed – illegally – and against the will of the majority of West Virginians.

## Appalachian Magazine

Founded in February 2014, *Appalachian Magazine* is a regionally owned publisher dedicated to telling Appalachia's story, then and now.

In addition to our website, www.AppalachianMagazine.com, we also produce a quarterly print-publication which is available through our website or wherever books are sold.

Follow us on social media:
**Facebook.com/AppalachianMagazine**

**Twitter: @AppalachianMag**

Jeremy T.K. Farley

Chapter
One

# A Tale of Two Virginias

As a small child it was always easy for me to know when we had entered West Virginia, that wild and wonderful land my father always seemed to speak about with an almost sacred reverence – it was just on the other side of the giant, four lane tunnel which tore through the bedrock of East River Mountain.

Growing up, my mother took great pains in teaching my sister and me the pathway to Heaven, but as far as my father was ever concerned, it ran north on Interstate 77.

Though we probably lived no more than twelve miles due south of the state line, there was, and remains to this day, an undeniable difference between the two peoples separated by the oversized mountain ridge.

To put it mildly, everything changes when you drive through that forty-year-old structure which both divides and connects the Richmond government from her estranged daughter in Charleston.

## The Geographic Divisions

When the God of Creation molded the landscapes of eastern and western Virginia, He erected a mountain barrier between the two regions, which helped to fuel an intra-state dispute that ended only when the two incompatible sections were under the authority of different state governments.

In addition to the wall of mountains which separated the Virginia plantations from the mountainous settlements of the West, the settlers themselves were different: their heritage, ancestries and ideologies were all distinctly unique.

Eastern Virginia was settled mainly by the English, whereas western Virginia, or at least northwestern Virginia, was developed by a plethora of nationalities, including the Germans, Scots-Irish, independent minded English and even Eastern Europeans.

Having different regions of the same state being settled by various people groups is not unique to early Virginia – almost all the American colonies were settled by pockets of nationals; however, what made West Virginia so different was that Virginia's western counties were prevented basic opportunities to interact with other cultures. This mountain barricade thwarted any opportunities for West Virginians to dissipate inside the giant American melting pot.

Shielded by an impermeable barrier that is the Alleghany Mountains, unique societies flourished for generations, often just a handful of miles from an entirely foreign culture.

It was this lack of personal contact which prevented a good understanding between the English inhabitants of eastern Virginia and the German, Scotch- Irish and other inhabitants of western Virginia. At any time previous to the Civil War a good system of canals and railroads would have gone far toward bringing the two parts of the Old Dominion more closely together; but the rulers in Richmond were blind to the importance of such improvements and the contest of 1861 dawned with eastern and western Virginia as widely apart in manners, customs, and sympathies as though thousands of miles intervened between them.

A survey of the chief geographical features of Virginia reveals that the surface of the state is divided into two unequally inclined planes and a centrally located valley. Virginia's lush and navigable landscape is comprised of fertile valleys bordered by stretching mountain ridges.

In contrast, the Mountain State's geography features countless steep mountains splotched together in an elaborate prehistoric maze.

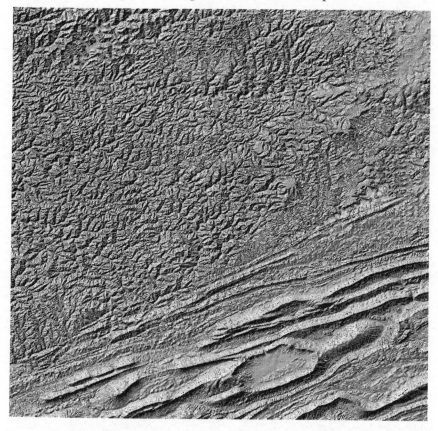

PHOTO: Topographical map of the West Virginia and Virginia border, near Bluefield. Notice West Virginia's (to the north) maze of mountains, compared to Virginia's (to the south) long mountain ridges and valleys. Photo Credit – USGS.

If it be true, as Washington once said, that people's faces are naturally turned in the direction of the flow of their rivers, then we may comprehend why misunderstandings were constantly arising, not only between the eastern and western Virginians, but also between the inhabitants of the smaller subdivisions of the old state. East of the Blue Ridge, the people follow their rivers to the east or the south;

the western Virginians looked out to the north or to the southwest. The commercial interests of the two great parts of Virginia were so dissimilar that when the war broke out in 1861 it was found that the two sections of Virginia had little commercial dependence upon each other.

## The Cultural Divisions

Long before the Revolutionary War, my ancestors and thousands of others, had forsaken eastern Virginia's commercial centers, pushing the colony's frontier farther and farther west.

At the age of 24, Thomas Beury Farley joined a garrison of 50 men who departed from Virginia's northeastern county of Albemarle. The group moved westward, first to what is known today as Greenbrier and then on to the New River.

The year was 1755 and their mission was to construct forts along the western frontier. The fortifications were to play a vital role in deterring Indian attacks upon early settlements in the region.

Virginia and her colonial neighbors were in the midst of a bloody war for western territory against an alliance comprised of French soldiers and Native Americans.

With the Old Dominion's vulnerable western settlements completely cutoff from militia forces in Richmond, protecting what is now West Virginia became a top priority of the English government.

The following year, English explorers tasted the murky waters of the Tug Fork River, the northern fork of the Big Sandy.

This tributary has been stained with the blood of lawmen, feuding neighbors and exploited workers for centuries.

Toponymist George R. Stewart writes about the origin of the name 'Tug Fork,' which serves as the modern-day border between West Virginia and Kentucky:

"In 1756 a small army of Virginians and Cherokees conducted war raids against the Shawnee. At one point they killed and ate two buffaloes and hung their hides on a tree. Later they returned and, being out of provisions, took the hides and cut them into thin strips called 'tugs.' These they roasted and ate. For this reason, the story goes, the stream was given the name 'Tug.'"[1][2]

---

[1] George R. Stewart. *Names on the Land*. Houghton Mifflin Company: Boston (1967).

Like the Kanawha, the Tug River cuts through the heart of the impenetrable mountains of West Virginia. The ancient waterways have provided the inhabitants of this difficult land a passageway to the Ohio River and America's heartland for eons.

It is because of these differences in watersheds that Virginians and West Virginians were often literally facing in different directions. Those living east of the Blue Ridge never stopped looking toward the sea, whereas those who had crossed the mountain ridges had no easy access to the ocean. Instead, their communications and visions were trained upon Pittsburgh, the Ohio Valley and the American Midwest.

It is then no surprise that West Virginia University competes in the Big XII Conference, today, or that Marshall University spent years in the Mid-American Conference; West Virginia has always been more of a Midwestern state than an East Coast state – no one just ever took notice of this reality.

PHOTO: The Tug Fork which flows into the Ohio River. West Virginia is on the right, Kentucky is on the left.
Photo Credit – Tim Kiser.

---

[2] Collins, Lewis (1877). *History of Kentucky*. p. 459.

## The Economic Divisions

The third and final marked difference between agrarian Virginia and her mountainous daughter were the economies of the two regions.

Nearly all of eastern Virginia was comprised solely of large-scale tobacco plantations. "Old Virginia," as she was often referred to as, was by and large poor in natural resources, negating nearly all types of land uses outside of farming.

The story for West Virginia, on the other hand, was quite the opposite.

The towering mountains blanketing the state made anything other than subsistence farming along tiny streams at the base of a mountain impossible.

What the region lacked in agriculture, however, it more than made up for in natural resources – valuable resources that would soon attract the lust of wealthy industrial barons who cared nothing about the people or the land of West Virginia.

The existence of coal in West Virginia had been known by European colonists since the mid-1700s. Early settlers to the region were even said to have extracted ground layers of the soft rock for use in heating their homes.

Still, the first large scale mining of coal in West Virginia did not begin until the early-1830s and existed merely as a support to the region's booming salt industry.

West Virginia's first true coal miners were slaves who extracted the mineral for use as a fuel to fire nearby salt furnaces. These furnaces were mostly located along the Kanawha River.

According to Ronald L. Lewis, professor of history emeritus at West Virginia University, "The erection of salt furnaces in Kanawha County beginning in 1797 provided the initial stimulus to coal mining. By 1840, 90 furnaces produced a million bushels of salt annually and consumed 200,000 tons of coal."[3]

Prior to the American Civil War, the demand for salt began to decline; however, bituminous coal (soft coal) had proven itself as being an economic alternative to burning wood.

---

[3] Lewis, Ronald L. "Coal Industry." e-WV: The West Virginia Encyclopedia. 19 June 2012. Web. 15 September 2015.

In the days leading up to the Lincoln Presidency, western Virginia coal was being used to power steamboats floating along the Ohio River, light coal oil lamps and power factories scattered across the northeast.

## Northern West Virginia vs. Southern West Virginia

Over the past century and a half, historians have been quick to point out the many differences which existed in the mid-1800s between western Virginia and eastern Virginia.

While it is true that the two regions shared undeniable distinctions, this oversimplification of the State of West Virginia's early history has led to several grossly inaccurate assumptions that have now been accepted as fact by the vast majority of Americans and even West Virginians.

Unfortunately, modern-day historians have all but neglected to even mention one of the greatest of divisions that existed in Western Virginia two centuries ago, a disunion which remains very real in present-day West Virginia: Northern West Virginia vs. Southern West Virginia.

Evidence of this disparity may be clearly seen simply by taking a stroll down the streets of Wheeling and Welch, Morgantown and Matewan, and Parkersburg and Princeton. The two regions of West Virginia could not be any more distant in economies, demographics and ancestry. In short, the same divisions that have always existed in Western Virginia remain today... in the State of West Virginia.

Today, just as was the case in the early 1860s, the people of the state's northern region domineer over the people of the state's southern section — perfect evidence of this can be seen in the fact that only one person in over 50 years from any place south of Charleston has been elected to serve as governor of the Mountain State.

When we look at early western Virginia's turbulent history, we must not see things as West vs. East, but as Northwest vs. East and Northwest vs. Southwest.

Sadly, the true culprit of the disruption of Virginia has never been dealt with and the economies and communities of southern West Virginia are worse off today than ever before in their histories.

## Southern West Virginia's Early Settlers

Following the French and Indian War, my 6x-great-grandfather, Thomas Buery Farley, moved his entire family to present-day Mercer County and then a few miles east to the banks of the New River in what is now Giles County, Virginia.

Nearly all of this region would become Southern West Virginia and be settled by men whose stories were very similar to my grandfather's.

They were descendants of early English settlers whose ancestors had braved the deadly winters of Jamestown and through an unmatched Anglican pride created the Colony of Virginia.

With adventure in their blood, the frontier their grandparents settled, had, over the course of a century, become too tamed for their tastes.

Filled with a hereditary zeal to find adventure, these descendants of Virginia's earliest white citizens pushed westward in pursuit of a land that was wild and wonderful. Settling the areas south of the Kanawha Valley, these were the first white men to call places such as Mercer, Monroe, Greenbrier, Raleigh, Fayette, Kanawha, Logan, Wyoming and McDowell counties home.

In an era where one's nationality was linked far more to their state or colony than the "united States," these early settlers were fiercely loyal to Virginia. They saw themselves as Virginians just as much as the modern-day inhabitants of these same places see themselves as Americans. Their grandparents had created Virginia and their drive westward was fueled in part by a desire to increase their homeland's influence and territory.

## Northern West Virginia's Early Settlers

While the great-great-great grandsons of Jamestown were busy settling the Tug and Kanawha Valleys, what would be seen by many in Richmond as a northern invasion into Virginia's sovereign territory had already quietly began just south of Pennsylvania.

In 1716 a Welsh Colonel who had spent years in Delaware and Pennsylvania crossed below what would become the Mason-Dixon Line and established one of the first permanent settlements in West Virginia. The man's name was Morgan Morgan and his sons would be credited for founding the City of Morgantown.

# West Virginia: The Illegal State

Unlike the settlers of southern West Virginia, Morgan had no allegiances to the Commonwealth of Virginia, instead, his loyalties were to Pennsylvania – in 1717 he was appointed as executor of the will of the Lieutenant Governor of Pennsylvania. Morgan was a Pennsylvanian and so were most of the settlers who followed in his steps, settling areas north of Charleston.

Between 1750 and 1800, small isolated settlements began to dot the borders of the state.

Emigration from the north to West Virginia was through Pennsylvania down the Ohio River or up the Monongahela and its tributaries. The movement was gradual and the settlements so scattered that as late as 1787 Jefferson's map of Virginia shows only two towns, Wheeling and Parkersburg, in the northern part of western Virginia.

After the Revolution, additional settlers began to pour into the state, so that by the mid-1800s, Western Virginia was a region whose populace was nearly equally divided — roughly half of its residents chose to fight for the South, while the other half elected to side with the Union.

Contrary to what most history books state, West Virginia was anything but a united state in the midst of the American Civil War and the vast majority of the residents of its southern counties were fiercely opposed to the creation of a new state from what was the Mother of States and Statesmen, the Old Dominion.

Once the idea of the State of West Virginia was made a reality, early leaders made it very plain that the northern region would rule over the rebel southern counties.

When it came time to establish the state's first public university in 1867, rather than place the college in a centrally located community, so that all West Virginians could be equally benefitted, northern leaders founded it less than ten miles from the Pennsylvania state line, completely out of reach for the state's southern and impoverished residents – their lot in life, it seemed, would be to serve as manual laborers, hewing down massive trees, digging hundreds of feet under the ground and enduring generational poverty. Educating "the peasantry of southern West Virginia" was viewed by many in the North with as much suspicion as teaching a slave to read a generation earlier.

Just as the Civil War placed Americans against Americans, the aftermath of this terrible and bloody war would place West Virginian against West Virginian for generations to come.

Their battles would be waged at Paint Creek, Matewan and Blair Mountain, as a corrupt and illegally formed state government sided with northern industrial tycoons over its own citizens.

Sadly, the rest of the country has moved on from the scars produced by the War Between the States, but southern West Virginia really has never been afforded this same luxury — though the state's residents have collectively blocked these wounds from their minds, the lasting damage done to the people of the mountains by the unlawful creation of West Virginia is obvious at every turn.

West Virginia is not a northern state and it is not a southern state. It is the watershed state, where east meets the mid-west and where the thick and snappy Pennsylvania accent gives way to the southern drawl. When studying the legality of the Mountain State and the events which transpired during and after the American Civil War, it is essential that we recognize the fact that West Virginia, as it exists today, has two separate histories, heritages and homelands – there is and has always been a Northern West Virginia and a Southern West Virginia. Failure to understand these two distinct regions create an inability to understand West Virginia.

## Where Did West Virginians Come From?

To put it simply, West Virginians are a different breed of people – and proud of it! They live differently, love differently and remember differently. They... We... cherish our state's remarkable and turbulent history. We were taught to appreciate the strength of our elders and grew up to treasure the stories of bloody mine wars, early settlers and grandma's pappy.

In West Virginia, history lives through the impoverished children who sat at their daddy's feet listening to stories of brave men and women who gladly laid down their lives for the principle of a matter.

Most early miners had nothing to leave to their children, nothing except for hundreds of stories and thousands of memories; yet these were the best inheritances any child could have ever hoped to receive. But where did these proud and formidable people come from?

It is impossible to trace with any degree of accuracy the movements of population in western Virginia.

From the North, early settlers emigrated from Pennsylvania.

In the infant-days of the American nation, the northern Panhandle grew rapidly, as the opening of the Mississippi River began to commercially rival the older settlements of the east.

South of the New River, known as the Little Kanawha, the people came mainly from Virginia.

By 1755, pioneers had pushed into the valley of the Greenbrier and spread out into all parts of the Great Kanawha Valley. The entire district west of the Blue Ridge was organized as Augusta County and the portion lying west of Hampshire County was commonly known as West Augusta.

Fincastle County was organized in 1772 and included all the present state of West Virginia lying between the Great Kanawha and the Big Sandy rivers.

At the outbreak of the Revolution it was estimated that there were 30,000 white people living within the boundaries of what is now West Virginia.

In 1790 the first census disclosed a population of approximately 59,000 whites in the nine counties lying wholly or partially in West Virginia. The increase of population from 1800 to the Civil War was swift and every year found the western counties growing both in size and importance.

The census of 1860 gave Virginia a population of 1,596,318, which made it the fifth most populous state in the Union.

Within the bounds of the present state of West Virginia, there were approximately 323,526 white persons and 28,256 slaves.

Though many other regions of the Mountain State were home to several thousand slaves, Wheeling and other communities along the Northern Panhandle had very few in comparison. The close proximity of free states such as Ohio and Pennsylvania made it almost unprofitable to own slaves in this peninsula of human bondage – a slave desiring to escape needed only run to freedom in one of three directions.

In the Northern Panhandle county of Ohio, at the outbreak of the Civil War, there were 5,511 persons of foreign birth, principally Irish and German, thus constituting one-seventh of the entire foreign-born population of the state.

In contrast with the Northern Panhandle are the southern counties of present-day West Virginia, places such as Logan,

McDowell, Mercer, Greenbrier, Raleigh and Monroe counties. The white population of these counties were almost entirely native-born Virginians, a people who were pleased to be subject to the government in Richmond. They were mountain men, self-reliant characters whose ancestors had crossed the Blue Ridge on purpose and reveled in the fact that the state government was hundreds of miles and several days away. They were libertarians in every sense of the word.

Though the layout of the land made the ownership of slaves impractical for most in places such as McDowell County, the map below, which provides the percentage of slave population by county, reveals that many West Virginia counties had significant levels of slave populations.

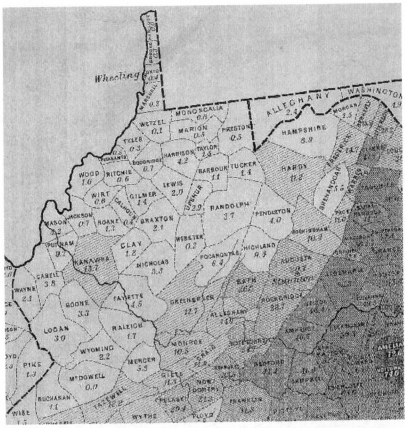

MAP: 1861 map showing the percentage of each Virginia county's population which were slaves.

According to the 1860 Census, nearly 14% of Kanawha County's total residents were slaves. More than one out of ten people living in the Western Virginia counties of Greenbrier and Hardy were also slaves.

These numbers pale in comparison, however, to West Virginia's Eastern Panhandle, which was also settled by Virginians: Berkeley County's slaves neared 19% of the locality's inhabitants and Jefferson County's total slave population equaled to more than one out of four people living in the county.

Thus on the great question of the day, the people of the two regions of Western Virginia were as widely apart as the earth's two poles.

The state's Northern Panhandle, settled by Pennsylvanians, were looking for an opportunity to break from the southern government, whereas West Virginia's southern and eastern counties saw no more reason to secede from the Richmond government than did places like Norfolk or Lynchburg.

## The Lasting Division

Today, as West Virginia struggles to realign its economy following what many in the state have referred to as a "war on coal," it may be hard for some to imagine, but once upon a time, real estate in the Mountain State was an invaluable commodity among investors.

As the nation neared the industrial revolution, the limitless resources of West Virginia's coal and timber seemed irresistible to many of the country's wealthiest companies and capitalists.

It is in part because of the state's irresistible wealth and the nefarious desires of many to loot this treasure that we believe the State of West Virginia was founded illegally, stolen from the people who settled the land; stolen through trickery, bribery and good o'le fashioned dirty West Virginia politics – all orchestrated by a northern junto government backed by many industrial tycoons.

The direct results of this coup d'état, which was fully realized on June 20, 1863, has been a century and a half of dirty government, suppression of the people and a total rewriting of history.

I am a West Virginian and my loyalty to the Mountain State is unwavering, it is home. With this said, it is time we as a people, learn our true history; For those who fail to learn from it are doomed to repeat it.

## A Tale of Two Virginias

The marked differences between the economies, qualities of life and general outlook between Old Virginia and West Virginia are sharp and undeniable.

I say this not poking fun at the Mountain State nor out of a desire to belittle the people or the place that I love so dearly, but rather as a matter of fact and with a hope that someone will make the conscientious decision to attack these problems at their root - a dishonest government.

Today, the Commonwealth of Virginia's unemployment rate hovers among the lowest in the nation, while that posted by the State of West Virginia ranks 51st of 50 states plus the District of Columbia... When it comes to jobs, we're last.[4]

On the subject of per capita incomes, Virginia is ranked eighth in the nation, while West Virginia places 47th out of 50 states.[5]

However, what I find to be most heartbreaking is this statistic comparing the life expectancies of residents living under the illegally created government which now sits in Charleston versus those who fall within the jurisdictional boundaries of the original capital of the mountains, Richmond.

According to the Centers for Disease Control and Prevention, the average person living in Virginia can expect to live to be 79-years-old, while the typical West Virginian is not expected to live past their 75th birthday – the 49th lowest life expectancy in the nation – "Thank God for Mississippi."

Sadly, the discrepancy between West Virginia and the Old Dominion is nothing new. The people of southern West Virginia have been, at the very worst, enslaved, and at the very best, exploited, almost as soon as the Mountain State was welcomed by the Lincoln Administration into the Union.

---

[4] "Unemployment Rates for States Monthly Rankings Seasonally Adjusted." U.S. Bureau of Labor Statistics. August 21, 2015. Web. 15 September 2015.
[5] "Per Capita Personal Income by State, 1990 to 2012." Bureau of Business & Economic Research, UNM. April 2, 2013. Web. 15 September 2015.

# Chapter Two

# Early Seeds of Disunion & Union

Following the American Revolution, an attitude of westward expansion emboldened many of the nation's pioneers to venture even farther into the dark forests which lay beyond the young Republic's mountain ridges.

Throughout most of early Virginia's history, its western settlers were seen as second class citizens. Referred to as "the peasantry of the West," the free people of the mountains withstood almost every political disadvantage the ruling elite of the Tidewater region could devise.

Nevertheless, the infant nation looked westward and Virginians were no exception.

In the twenty years that followed 1790, Harrison County, located in West Virginia's north-central region, increased in population from 2,080 to 9,958; Ohio County from 5,212 to 8,175; Pendleton County from 2,452 to 4,234; Randolph from 951 to 2,854.

Despite the exponential growth of these counties, the Virginia General Assembly refused to provide for the proportionate increase of representation in the House of Delegates. This refusal to grant fair representation in the Commonwealth of Virginia's legislative branch enabled the easternmost counties to retain the balance of power for generations and planted seeds of unrest and resentment across the hills of northern Western Virginia.

Forty-nine counties adjacent to each other in the eastern and southern sections of the state had a majority of the whole number of representatives in the most numerous branch of the legislature despite having 72,138 fewer free citizens.

On the other hand, the Virginia Senate was comprised of twenty-four members elected from senatorial districts, and in the course of time, the shifting of population had rendered the old grouping of counties as much out of date as was the system of representation in the lower house.

In 1810, 212,036 white persons of Virginia were represented by four Senators (1 senator per 53,009 residents), while in another part of the state thirteen Senators were chosen by a white population of 162,717 (1 senator per 12,516 residents).

## The Advantage of Living in Western Virginia

A lot has been stated in the +150 years following West Virginia's secession about the political disadvantage members of the western portion of the state underwent in relation to their eastern counterparts.

As proven in the section above, many of these disadvantages were very real; however, it is critical that the student of the Mountain State's early history realize that living on the great divide just beyond the valley also carried with it certain political advantages – the greatest of these was that the average West Virginian was far more likely to be a qualified voter than someone of equal stature east of the mountains:

Throughout early America, simply being a white male was not enough to earn the right to vote. The vast majority of states, including Virginia, required voters to be "freeholders," meaning landowners.

In early Virginia, the price of land came at a premium and was possessed largely by generational descendants of the state's earliest aristocracy.

President Thomas Jefferson, who also served as Governor of Virginia, once declared that "the majority of the men in the state who pay and fight for its support are unrepresented in the legislature."[6]

According to the President, more than half of the men "on the roll of the militia or of the tax gatherers" were not entitled to vote in the Commonwealth.

In one company of eighty Virginians fighting in the War of 1812, there was only one voter.

Beyond the Blue Ridge Mountains, however, land was cheap and plentiful. One wealthy eastern Virginian complained, "one might qualify as a freeholder for a very small sum of money."

In the west, a certain quantity of land may not have been worth five cents in all, while in the east the smallest quantity of land allowing the same privilege was worth from fifty to one hundred dollars.

The persons most discriminated against were the leaseholders, the mechanics and tradesmen of the cities, as well as the small farmers of the east. These, rather than the yeomen of the west, had reason to complain of electoral injustice. Nevertheless, it is from the West that the cry of oppression is most frequently remembered.

## Geographic Disunion

As is true with most historical events of great magnitude, it seems as if the course for dividing Virginia from her mountainous daughter to the west had been predestined since the very foundations of the earth were lain.

---

[6] Thomas Jefferson, Henry Augustine Washington. *The Works of Thomas Jefferson: Published by Order of Congress* (1884). p. 360.

In addition to the political walls of disunion that were erected by Tidewater farmers, the two peoples' greatest barrier were the mountains themselves.

It is not to be said, however, that numerous great schemes from representatives of both sides of the mountains were never attempted in order to bring together the mountain-severed peoples of Old Virginia.

A note of alarm was sounded officially in 1857 – After complaining that the products of Western Virginia were being sent to Pennsylvania, Ohio, and Louisiana, one observer declared the following: "By every geographical and geological cause were our people segregated into separate communities and divided from each other and all mutual commercial dependency."[7]

## An Impossible Barrier

Virginia's 33rd Governor, Henry A. Wise, who served from 1856 to 1860, correctly described the difficulties which would present themselves to workers who endeavored to pierce the mountain ranges with rails:

Connecting the Ohio River region by rail to the state's eastern tracks would require one to "pass over or through a backbone of, from one to two hundred miles, of mountains running in parallel ridges northeast and southwest across her entire limit. Tunnel after tunnel at short intervals arrest her progress and make each work one of patient labor and of time. She has to overcome a summit level of nearly 2,000 feet for a breadth from east to west; which no other people on the continent, any more than Virginians, have as yet overcome."[8]

Governor Wise was all too familiar with these hurdles, as numerous attempts to construct a railroad across, through, or around the imposing chains of mountains had been attempted and failed on many occasions in the days leading up to the American Civil War.

---

[7] James Dunwoody Brownson De Bow. *DeBow's Review, Volume 23* (1857). p. 60.

[8] James Dunwoody Brownson De Bow. *DeBow's Review, Volume 23* (1857). p. 64.

# Connecting by Canal

Out of all the early colonies, the only state whose geography created a conundrum that could even be comparable to Virginia's was that of the State of New York's.

Though not nearly as formidable as the Blue Ridge, New York's Adirondack Mountains effectively separate large portions of the state from its eastern commercial hub, New York City.

Fearful that such a division would prove to be a cause for fracture, the solution devised by state leaders was to build a canal that would enable navigation from New York City to the state's capital city of Albany and then to the state's far western boundary at Buffalo.

With construction beginning on July 4, 1817, the canal was completed eight years later in October 1825.

Constructing the 363-mile system cost $7million and has been hailed as one of the greatest engineering marvels of the nineteenth century.

Though pricey, historians make the case that the canal may have saved New York from the same fragmentation Virginia suffered, as well as helped solidify New York City as the world's center for commerce and trade.


## The Chesapeake & Ohio Canal

In the years following completion of the Erie Canal, leaders in Virginia sat out to build a series of canals in their own state, linking secluded areas of the Appalachians to markets along the Atlantic shoreline.

The first of these attempted canals was the Chesapeake & Ohio Canal. The goal of this undertaking was to link the waters of the Potomac with the Monongahela rivers, thus linking the Potomac to Pittsburgh.

Work on the proposed 185-mile canal began in 1828, but by 1850 only 50-miles had been completed, linking the Potomac to Cumberland, Maryland.

With the proposal of 74 canal locks, 11 aqueducts crossing major streams and more than 240 culverts to cross smaller streams, Virginia leaders realized very quickly the significant level of challenges constructing a major canal in the Appalachians would present.

The most notable feature of the canal was the 3,118 ft. Paw Paw Tunnel, constructed in Allegany County, Maryland.

Built to bypass six miles of consecutive horseshoe bends, the Paw Paw Tunnel took roughly fourteen years to complete and highlighted the racial differences that would soon tear the region apart.

According to Thomas F. Hahn, author of *Towpath Guide to the C&O Canal*, Lee Montgomery, a Methodist minister who was experienced in constructing canal tunnels was awarded the contract on March 15, 1836.

Construction on the tunnel began that same year, unfortunately, the Irish workers Montgomery hired were not skilled at tunnel work and quickly

The view of the east side entrance to the Paw Paw Tunnel on the C & O Canal Towpath

fell into sectarian strife with English and Welsh miners.

"More unfortunately, this caused racial tensions which exploded into violence in 1837 and 1838, specifically between the Irish and everyone else; destroying the tavern at Oldtown, burning shanties, and the like. There were more riots in 1839 at Little Orleans. Montgomery succeeded in boring the tunnel through on June 5, 1840, at a point 1505 feet from the south portal, but did not finish it."[9]

---

[9] "Paw Paw Tunnel." Wikipedia. February 18, 2015. Web. 18 September 2015.

Financial problems forced the construction of the tunnel to come to a halt from 1841 to 1847, before additional capital could be raised.

Once the tunnel was finally constructed, canal investors elected to call it quits and ended the canal at Cumberland, Maryland. The planned section to the Ohio River at Pittsburgh was never built.

This plan did not result in anything especially beneficial to Virginia and it may be doubted if the completion of the canal from Cumberland, Maryland, to the Monongahela would have positively impacted the relationship between Western Virginia and Old Virginia.

It is probable that its effect would have been similar to that of the Baltimore & Ohio Railroad — that is, the diversion of western trade to Baltimore rather than to Richmond.

## James River & Kanawha Canal

An even more audacious undertaking by early Virginia leaders was the James River & Kanawha Canal, a plan that would in essence link the Ohio River and all of Western Virginia to the Atlantic Ocean.

Had this plan been realized, there is little doubt that the history of the United States would have been incredibly different – specifically that of Western Virginia's.

The original proposal was first surveyed by George Washington and work began in 1785.

Intended to facilitate shipments of passengers and freight by water between the western counties of Virginia and the coast, the expensive project suffered numerous setbacks due to a lack in funding and flood damage.

Though largely financed by the Commonwealth of Virginia through the Virginia Board of Public Works, it was only half completed by 1851, some 65 years after work first began; Reaching the town of Buchanan in Botetourt County, roughly 60 miles from the canal's intended target, the New River (the south fork of the Kanawha).

Ultimately, the mountains of Virginia's spine were simply too costly and difficult to penetrate with a canal.

Furthermore, tough questions remained unanswered – if the James River was this difficult to canal, how much more problematic would the steep ravines, canyons and white water rapids would the New River pose?

General Assembly records from 1829-30 reveal that the canal – a project intended to unite the separated regions was having the opposite effect:

The western members of the assembly were accused of making an attempt to swamp the state with a mountain of debt for an impossible project that – even if it were ever realized – would only benefit the western region of the state.

Even in Western Virginia, there was no unity. The northern counties such as Monongahela and her neighbors were opposed to the James & Kanawha Canal, fearing that the project would rob funding from their canal, the Chesapeake & Ohio.

Unfortunately for the preservation of Virginia, leaders in Richmond, Morgantown and Wheeling failed to grasp the value of connecting the James and Kanawha rivers.

The map on this page has darkened every county in West Virginia and Virginia that either drains into the James or Ohio River.

Had the canal been completed, the Commonwealth of Virginia – West and East – would be linked to both the Atlantic Ocean and the Mississippi River: the possibilities and awesome economic power this would have created for local residents of the two Virginias are unimaginable!

Unfortunately, lack of foresight among leaders in Northern West Virginia and Eastern Virginia stifled this project.

MAP: West Virginia & Virginia counties with at least a portion of their watershed linking to the Ohio or James Rivers

Had the New, Kanawha, Big Sandy, Ohio and James ever linked, who can say how the history of Virginia, the Civil War and even that of America been changed?

32

Virginia's early leaders allowed the golden opportunity to slip by with but feeble attempts to carry out the projected scheme, and when the Civil War broke out, the canal had been completed only as far as Botetourt County, some nineteen miles northeast of Roanoke.

Despite the sectional differences, there were several voices of reasoning, as one annual report from 1860 records a recommendation that the General Assembly lay aside all petty jealousies and pass a bill for the union of the James and the Kanawha rivers, "and thus complete one of the grandest schemes that has engaged the attention of the country since the proposition of the Erie Canal."[10]

Unfortunately, these voices of optimism were quickly drowned out by the thumping drums of war as the nation prepared for civil anarchy and battle.

The program was scrapped in the town of Buchanan, having never left the James River watershed.

## Crises & Constitution Conventions

Out of all the early colonies-turned states, no settlement faced as many challenges as the Commonwealth of Virginia.

With its short-lived Fincastle County stretching as far west as modern-day Wisconsin, Virginia's early geography naturally created a situation in which its western inhabitants felt isolated from the state government in Richmond.

In just a handful of years, Fincastle County was broke into several smaller subdivisions and the Commonwealth of Kentucky was admitted into the Union on June 1, 1792 – decreasing the Old Dominion's western boundaries to the Ohio River.

### The Staunton Convention

The sectional troubles plaguing early Virginia reached a boiling point in 1816 and a series of meetings would be held by western politicians in an attempt to rectify the problem – these meetings would come to be known as the Staunton Convention.

---

[10] James Dunwoody Brownson De Bow. *DeBow's Review, Volume 28* (1860). p. 102.

Held for the purpose of changing the Virginia Constitution, thirty-seven counties lying between the Blue Ridge and the Ohio River were represented by seventy delegates.

In this convention, Botetourt, Rockbridge, Augusta, and Montgomery counties (modern-day Virginia's western counties) favored merely a mild petition to the legislature urging a redistricting of the state, whereas delegates from the counties farther west felt the need for a stronger method of persuasion and were willing to go to any length to accomplish their purpose.

Their chief ambition was to amend the state constitution "so as to give a fair and equal representation to every part of the state in both branches of the legislature."[11]

Unfortunately for the union of Virginia, the Staunton Convention of 1816 only succeeded in driving a wedge between the Old Dominion's western counties — revealing a staunch difference between the milder Blue Ridge communities and their stronger-willed mountainous counterparts farther to the west.

The convention adjourned after drawing up a memorial to the General Assembly using "the mildest language."

Far-western Virginia delegates were especially upset with a clause that described the existing inequalities in representation as an "operation of natural causes," instead, in true West Virginia fashion, they favored boldly decrying the evils perpetrated upon them by those in the far-east of the Commonwealth.

In the years ahead, beginning in 1817, numerous bills would be introduced into the General Assembly providing for the calling of a constitutional convention for the purpose of redressing certain wrongs which were inevitable under the old constitution.

Sometimes these bills passed the lower house only to be defeated in the state's Senate.

## A False Hope: 1829 Constitutional Convention

The plight of Virginia's West continued through the coming decade as the men of the mountains continued to fight for fair and proportionate representation in their state's government.

---

[11] *Nile's Weekly Register, Volume 11 (Saturday, September 7, 1816)*

Undaunted by their numerous defeats, the residents of Western Virginia finally succeeded in 1828 in putting the question of calling a constitutional convention to a referendum vote.

The residents of the Commonwealth approved the constitutional convention by a margin of 21,896 to 16,646 – even in spite of the fact that seven of eight voters from the Tidewater district voted in opposition to the measure.

The vote along what is now Virginia's I-81 corridor was overwhelmingly in favor of the convention, as were the results in present-day West Virginia, where 75% of the qualified voters expressed their approval.

Unwilling to surrender their stronghold on power without a fight, the ruling regime living near Virginia's eastern coastlines met in the General Assembly on February 10, 1829, and devised yet another obstacle to providing equal representation to the settlers of the West.

Writing the rules for the Virginia Constitutional Convention of October 1829, eastern delegates prescribed that each senatorial district was awarded four representatives to serve in the convention.

"That this plan worked to the advantage of the eastern counties," writes one historian, "may be seen from the fact that of the ninety-six delegates to the convention, forty-eight were from the Tidewater, twenty from the Piedmont, and twenty-eight from the Valley and the Trans- Alleghany."[12]

As the two older sections of the state were one on all important questions, particularly when their political primacy was at stake, the result was to give eastern Virginia sixty-eight of the ninety-six delegates in the convention. Stated more graphically, 362,745 white inhabitants in the Tidewater and Piedmont elected sixty-eight delegates (1 delegate per 5,334 residents) and 319,518 white persons in the Valley and Trans-Alleghany were represented by twenty-eight delegates (1 delegate per 11,411 residents).

Several eastern senatorial districts contained fewer than 20,000 whites, while the western senatorial districts, entitled to the same number of representatives, four, had a population of from 37,000 to 60,000.

The result of the Constitutional Convention was anything but relief for the people of the West and Blue Ridge Valley, as the

---

[12] James C. McGregor. *Disruption of Virginia* (1922). p. 34.

Convention failed to meet any of the grievances laid forth at the start of the meetings.

## Constitutional Convention of 1851

Finally, the long awaited relief for Western Virginia came in 1851, seventy-five years following the nation's declared independence.

Achieving this liberation can be directly attributed to changing demographics.

The Census of 1840 revealed a troubling reality for leaders of Virginia's east: the majority of the state's white residents and voters lived in the western regions of the Commonwealth.

This transformation in power made it impossible for the state's eastern gentry to ignore the voice of its West any longer – they would soon be returning to the bargaining table of a Constitutional Convention and this time, the East would be ready to negotiate.

Underrepresented in the General Assembly, the western citizens began to openly discuss secession from the Old Dominion, causing alarm for leaders in Richmond.

In an effort to keep the state together and protect the establishment of slavery, the politicians from the East sat down with representatives from the West, ready to make considerable concessions.

The 1851 Virginia Constitution made radical changes to the structure of the state's government – proving to be overwhelmingly favorable to the residents beyond the Blue Ridge in what is today West Virginia.

Changes to the state's government included:
a.) **Universal white male suffrage**
   *no longer would owning property be a requirement for voting*
b.) **The election of Governor, Lt. Governor and judges by popular vote**
   *as opposed to the state legislature, which had previously been choosing these officers*

In exchange for what can only be seen as major victories, the representatives of Western Virginia conceded not to abolish voice voting in exchange for secret ballot voting in elections.

A second concession was made concerning the ever increasingly divisive issue of slavery:

The West Virginia Encyclopedia quotes Louis H. Manarin, as stating, "To appease Eastern slaveholders, the property tax rate on slaves was set lower than on land and livestock."[13]

Approved by a vote of 75 to 33, the new Virginia Constitution was submitted to the voters in October 1851 and was approved by 87.3% of the voters (75,748 votes for and 11,060 against).

With its widespread acceptance throughout the Commonwealth, the Constitution of 1851 gave Virginians on both sides of the mountain cause for hope and optimism.

With the nation teetering on the brink of total disunion throughout the 1850s, the Commonwealth of Virginia enjoyed greater unity in its entire history during this decade, as leaders and politicians on both sides of the Blue Ridge Mountains felt their needs had been met by the Constitution of 1851.

Virginia was united for the first time in its history.

---

[13] Manarin, Louis H. "Constitution of 1851." e-WV: The West Virginia Encyclopedia. 07 February 2011. Web. 18 September 2015.

## Chapter Three

# The Election of Abraham Lincoln

With the Virginia Constitution of 1851 having been in effect for nearly a decade on the day Americans went to the polls in November 1860, the people of western Virginia were overwhelmingly satisfied – at least on a local level – with the great progress that had been made in burying the hatchet between West Virginia and East Virginia.

Both sides had made important concessions and both regions had garnered great gains following the convention – the greatest winner, however, was the common man or at least the common white man, as the new constitution provided for universal suffrage for all white men, regardless of whether or not they owned property.

## Election of 1860

The American Presidential Election of 1860 was one that featured four major candidates for the nation's highest office, Abraham Lincoln, Stephen Douglas, John Breckinridge and John Bell.

Each of these men enjoyed varying degrees of success throughout the South except for Lincoln, who failed to carry a single county south of the Ohio River – including each of the localities that would become West Virginia.

The inescapable issue of the election was slavery and in particular, its expansion.

Lincoln, the Republican Party's first candidate for President was well known for being adamantly opposed to the very institution and had on more than one occasion called for its termination.

John C. Breckinridge, a Kentucky native and sitting Vice President was selected to represent the southern wing of the Democratic Party. He was pro-Southern, pro-Slavery and pro-Secession if the need should arise.

Illinois' Stephen Douglas, on the other hand, was seen as a more moderate candidate and was chosen by the Democratic Party's northern faction.

Tennessean John Bell also tossed his hat into the ring for the Presidency, running for the office on the ticket of the newly created Constitutional Union Party. Bell, however, failed to offer a party platform and chose not speak on any controversial issues during what was the most critical election in the nation's history – opting instead to walk a very fragile line in appealing to voters in both the Deep South and Union North.

Despite not taking a true stand on any of the issues, Bell polled fairly well throughout all of the south and squeaked by with a victory in Virginia in what remains to this day, the closest presidential election in the Commonwealth's history – winning over Breckinridge by only 156 votes out of 166,891 total ballots cast.

## The Entire State Votes

Thanks to the Constitution of 1851, all free white men in Virginia were provided the opportunity to vote in this election.

Due to the fact that every free Virginia male was given an opportunity to vote in the state's election, we must accept the results of the election as a reasonably accurate portrayal of the state's sentiments regarding the pressing issue at hand, namely slavery, state's rights and Abraham Lincoln.

## A United Virginia

Despite their turbulent history and decades of regional differences, Virginians had risen above many of the root causes of the sectional strife which had defined the state's earlier years of existence.

The success of the Constitution of 1851 had provided a fresh opportunity for leaders from both the East and the West to move forward in creating a new era in the history of the Commonwealth of Virginia and for nearly a decade, they had been doing just that.

By Tuesday, November 6, 1860, Virginians, both from the West and the East, were united as one people – at least in their opposition to one Presidential candidate, Abraham Lincoln.

The below map displays in gray and black the individual counties won by Abraham Lincoln in his first presidential bid (the darker the county, the greater Lincoln's margin of victory).

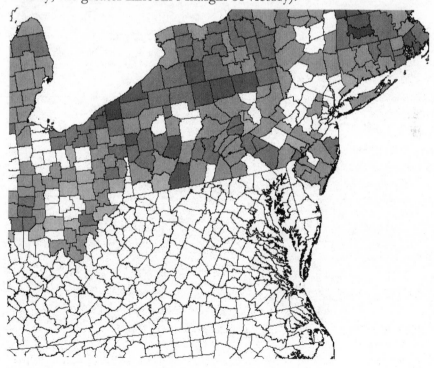

This election map on the previous page completely destroys the popular, albeit false, narrative that has been presented to the American public in the years following the state's establishment – the notion that western Virginians were staunch supporters of Abraham Lincoln and that the general populace was so loyal to him that when it came time, they chose to sever all ties with their brethren to the east in allegiance to the newly installed President from Illinois.

In reality, the voting population of western Virginia was just as opposed to the prospect of a Lincoln Presidency as their counterparts in the Tidewater region along the Atlantic Coast.

## West Virginia:
## The Region Won by the "Southern Extremist"

John C. Breckinridge served as the Antebellum South's candidate of choice, favoring slavery at all costs, even at the expense of the Union, whereas Bell, who won Virginia, appealed to a more moderate electorate.

Interestingly, Breckinridge actually fared better in the counties that would become West Virginia than in what is present-day Virginia. Though he lost the Old Dominion and its 15 electoral votes, the South's candidate of choice actually carried the future counties of the Mountain State, winning that region by nearly two percentage points.

| Presidential Election of 1860 in Virginia | | | | | | |
|---|---|---|---|---|---|---|
| Candidate | TOTAL | | Modern-Day Virginia | | Modern-Day West Virginia | |
| John Bell | **74,681** | 44.7% | 53,684 | 45.8% | 20,997 | 42.0% |
| John C. Breckinridge | **74,323** | 44.4% | 52,415 | 44.7% | 21,908 | 43.8% |
| Stephen Douglas | **16,290** | 9.7% | 10,548 | 9.0% | 5,742 | 11.5% |
| Abraham Lincoln | **1,929** | 1.2% | 527 | 0.4% | 1,402 | 2.8% |

In total, 167,223 Virginians cast their ballots in the Presidential Election of 1860, the most in the state's history up to that point.

Of the more than 167,000 men who announced their choice for president across Virginia on that crisp November morning, only 1,887 proclaimed a vote for Abraham Lincoln, 1.2% of the total number of voters.

Though Lincoln polled best in the counties of the Northern Panhandle, which include Hancock, Brooke, Ohio and Marshall, he failed to obtain a majority in any county – not even earning a single vote in Marshall County, which is bordered by the State of Ohio on its western flank and the State of Pennsylvania to its east.

Ultimately, the winning candidates from each of the Northern Panhandle's counties were the same individuals who carried the Deep South.

Just as all the counties of North Carolina, Texas and Mississippi had done, the counties of the Northern Panhandle gave the majority of their votes to either Bell or Breckinridge.

## A Minority in Three Counties Re-Write History

Though he failed to claim victory in a single Northern Panhandle county, Lincoln did poll better in this region than anywhere else in the state:

| County | Lincoln Votes | Total Votes |
|--------|---------------|-------------|
| Hancock | 254 | 634 |
| Brooke | 173 | 872 |
| Ohio | 771 | 3,604 |
| **Total** | **1,198** | **5,110** |

Out of Lincoln's 1,929 votes received in Virginia in 1860, 1,198 (62%) of them came from the three most northern counties of the panhandle.

His remaining 731 votes came from tiny pockets of abolitionists scattered throughout Virginia, including 55 in the eastern Virginia county of Prince William and another 40 from Fairfax and Alexandria.

The combined cumulative total of all Lincoln votes cast in Virginia in the Election of 1860 equates to 1.2%. If we remove the state's three northernmost counties, that percentage drops to a dismal half of one percent – statewide, including eastern and western Virginia.

Even in the Ohio County community of Wheeling, a place that has established a reputation for being at the forefront of abolitionism, Lincoln failed to place any higher than third out of four candidates for President.

Nevertheless, the storyline has been told and retold so long that people, including West Virginians, believe it: The narrative which states that the citizens of the West were worlds apart politically in 1860 from their cousins in the East. So different in fact, that a bitter divorce was the only solution to end their marital difficulties.

As the voting map and election results point out, however, the people of West Virginia (outside of its three most northern counties) were just as anti-Lincoln as the people of the East and just as united as a single populace as any state in the union.

By the end of the 1850s, leaders from both sides of the Blue Ridge had matured and found ways to improve upon relations, so much so that apart from a tiny pocket living in extreme-Northwestern Virginia, the Commonwealth of Virginia was united going into the new year of 1861.

Unfortunately for the inhabitants of this state's western counties, the forces lurking in the shadows would soon be instituting a coup d'état, usurping the will of the voters and sending a free and industrious people on a collision course with poverty that would continually worsen over the next 150 years.

Little could the men of Calhoun County, who gave Breckinridge 93% of their total vote, Pocahontas County who sided 333 to 163 for Breckridge, or Logan County, whom the southern candidate carried 72% of the electorate, have imagined that within two and a half years' time, supporters of a candidate who received fewer than 2,000 votes out of +167,000 ballots cast statewide would be running their state and convincing subsequent generations that the illegal government reigning over them was the will of the people.

## West Virginia, the Slave State

In this chapter, the reader has been confronted with several undeniable facts.

Among these facts are:

1.) West Virginians elected the more hardline, pro-slavery, pro-secessionist candidate, compared to their eastern brothers

2.) Abraham Lincoln carried only 2.8% of the vote in what would become modern-day West Virginia.
(*If we remove the state's three northernmost counties, that percentage drops to a dismal half of one percent*)

These two statements beg the question, "Why?"

Why did West Virginia so overwhelmingly reject the one candidate opposed to slavery? Why did they choose the pro-slavery Dixie candidate?

Sadly, the answer to this question is fairly simple, West Virginia was a slave state, in fact, West Virginia was the last slave state to be admitted into the Union and the last place in America where slavery was permitted by Federal law.

Like so many other American school children from my generation, my teachers provided me with a very limited expose on the American Civil War and the amount of time dedicated to telling the history of West Virginia was even less.

The short narrative was always something along the following lines:

"At the outbreak of the American Civil War, the eastern portion of Virginia, whose land was far more conducive to large-scale plantations, voted to secede from the Union and join the Confederacy. The state's western counties were opposed to slavery and so, naturally, they elected to form their own abolitionist state, the State of West Virginia."

Though very brief, the above paragraph accurately sums up the typical American and even the average West Virginian's understanding of how and why the Mountain State was founded.

In all truthfulness, however, the American Civil War is an extremely complicated subject and contains tens of thousands of nuances, motives, fears and incentives for why certain people, communities, states, and organizations chose the side they did.

Also, we must not forget that the Confederate States of America was, at least initially, a confederation, a loose alliance of sovereign states – each one of which had its own unique purpose for entering the fight.

As we will reveal in the pages ahead, Virginia's reasoning for entering the war on the side of Dixie may have been entirely different from Georgia's and Wheeling's decision to enter the war on the side of the North was undoubtedly different than Massachusetts's objectives.

Unfortunately, reality for tens of thousands of black Americans living west of the Blue Ridge Mountains was something far different than the popular and commonly accepted narrative – the counties of West Virginia were, right up to the close of the Civil War, home to countless slaves. Even worse, the slave population in West Virginia had risen by more than 26% between the years of 1820 and 1850.[14]

As was mentioned at the close of Chapter One, according to the 1860 Census, nearly 14% of Kanawha County's total residents were slaves and other West Virginia counties had slave populations between 19-25%.

Though it is true that slavery west of Virginia's Blue Ridge Mountains was not nearly as predominate, the fact remains, that West Virginia was a place where slavery existed and in many places on a grand scale.

Though these facts are all well documented pieces of American history, somewhere over the past +150 years these truths have for the most part escaped mention in our history books and school classroom lectures; children can now complete twelve years of public education and never lay eyes on any more than a handful of total pages dedicated to the Civil War.

Perhaps what is even more astonishing to the average person is this: slavery legally ended in Virginia before it did in West Virginia.

That's right, slavery in places under Confederate control in the Commonwealth of Virginia, was made officially illegal on January 1, 1863, when President Abraham Lincoln gave the Emancipation Proclamation, calling for the freeing of all slaves thereafter captured by Union soldiers. For the state government in Wheeling, rife with birthing pains, President Lincoln provided a special exemption in the

---

[14] United States Census Data

46

actual text of his famous Emancipation Proclamation, exempting them from the demand:

*"Now, therefore I, Abraham Lincoln, President of the United States, by virtue of the power in me vested as Commander-in-Chief, of the Army and Navy of the United States in time of actual armed rebellion against the authority and government of the United States, and as a fit and necessary war measure for suppressing said rebellion, do, on this first day of January, in the year of our Lord one thousand eight hundred and sixty-three, and in accordance with my purpose so to do publicly proclaimed for the full period of one hundred days, from the day first above mentioned, order and designate as the States and parts of States wherein the people thereof respectively, are this day in rebellion against the United States, the following, to wit:*

*"Arkansas, Texas, Louisiana… Mississippi, Alabama, Florida, Georgia, South Carolina, North Carolina, and Virginia, (except the forty-eight counties designated as West Virginia… And by virtue of the power, and for the purpose aforesaid, I do order and declare that all persons held as slaves within said designated States, and parts of States, are, and henceforward shall be free; and that the Executive government of the United States, including the military and naval authorities thereof, will recognize and maintain the freedom of said persons."*

The reality is this, West Virginia's early history is far more complex than most have ever realized or been taught!

## Slavery in Wheeling

In the days leading up to the American Civil War, Wheeling, Virginia, grew into an important stop along the underground railroad, standing as it does between Ohio and Pennsylvania.

Many runaway slaves would enter into the city by darkness of night and find lodging courtesy of the A.M.E. Zion Church and the proprietor of the Wheeling House Hotel, who would arrange safe houses for runaways.

One local family, the McKeever's, would hide fugitive slaves in their poultry wagon and drive them to freedom in Pittsburgh.

Despite these gems of humanity, the City of Wheeling also has a very dark and shameful history – one in which slavery not only existed but was a lucrative industry.

At the epicenter of slavery in this peninsula of bondage, which stretched farther north than Staten Island, was the Wheeling Market House, a place where weekly slave auctions were held.

Located along the National Road and on the banks of the Ohio River, Wheeling, Virginia, was ideally suited for slave trade, as purchased individuals would often be barged down the Ohio to places in the Deep South.

Nineteenth century historian Thomas B. Seabright wrote: "Negro slaves were frequently seen on the National Road. They were driven over the road arranged in couples and fashioned to a long, thick rope, or cable, like horses."[15]

PHOTO: Wheeling Market House, location of weekly slave auctions

---

[15] Thomas B. Searight. *The Old Pike. A History of the National Road* (1894). p. 109.

Joseph Bell, born in 1819, remembered seeing on Wheeling streets, "gangs of slaves chained together, women as well as men, on their way south. As a little boy, I remember standing on the sidewalk with my brother when such a gang was passing. We were eating an ear of corn apiece, which some of the slaves begged from us."

According to historians, the ringing of the market bell would signify to the community of Wheeling that a slave trade was about to begin.[16]

Judge John Cochran, an Ohio abolitionist, wrote of one of his early visits to a Wheeling slave auction as a young child:

*Saturday morning in June while attending this market at the age of ten years and while gratifying our idle curiosities as boys will sometimes do, I with a neighbor boy sauntered to the upper end of the markethouse and there beheld a sight which I shall never forget and which afterwards changed my whole political thought and action. It was a slave auction.*

*The auction block was on the west side of the upper end of the market about where the city scales are now located. It was a wooden movable platform about two and a half feet high and six feet square approached by some three or four steps. The auctioneer was a little dapper fellow with a ringing voice and an air of self-important bustle which to a boy bespoke him a man of surprising importance. Not a very large crowd was surrounding the auction block. On top of it was a portly and rather aged negress and the auctioneer. She was a mulatto had a broad full face a soft matronly eye and gray hair. Her look was all kindness and affection though now it wore a sad and troubled expression, I liked her as soon as I saw her.*

*Grouped together on the ground at the side of the block stood three other negroes two men and one woman. They were all about the same age the woman, being probably two years younger than the men and aged about twenty. She was also a mulatto, as was one of the*

---

[16] MARGARET BRENNAN "Slavery Alive and Well in Wheeling." Sunday News-Register, The Intelligencer / Wheeling News-Register. 4 March 2012. Web. 18 September 2015.

49

*men, while the other who was her brother was quite dark with features and expression like his mother on the auction block. In outline of form and face the girl looked like her mother and darker brother though here as to the brother the resemblance ended. She was tall and slender with a queenly grace and voluptuous swell of chest and gave evidence of refinement not looked for in a slave. Her lips were thin as those of a white person and her eyes quite dark. They were full of tears.*

*I thought her lovely. She was almost white and her hair while wavy was not short and tight curled like her brother's, but long and jet black. Had she been in Spain, no question would have been made that she was a Spaniard.*

*In my childish innocence, I could not reason how this girl could be the sister of that black brother. Subsequent knowledge has taught me my mistake, though only half a mistake after all. It arose from the conditions of American slavery. What a contradiction of words 'American slavery.' And yet it was true!*

*Then her head fell again and when I quietly slipped around in front of her and looked up into her face the tears were freely rolling over her cheeks down onto her blue checked apron. I knew something was wrong and I wanted to give relief. I pulled the coat tail of an elderly gentleman and when he stooped down to know what I wanted he answered my inquiry by saying this was a slave auction and they were going to sell these four colored people.*

*He told me they would likely be purchased by different buyers and be separated for life — that the woman on the block was the mother of the black man and mulatto girl and that the other mulatto man and they all belonged to one master who had broken up and they were being sold to pay creditors. This elderly gentleman seemed so kind. He had a light brown broad brimmed hat and was dressed in drab colored clothes with clean white shirt and close fitting standing collar. His coat came up and fastened close to the neck like that of a minister He seemed educated and refined. His clothes, I noticed, had some flour on them. When he began to talk to me I saw at once he was a Quaker and for the first time I looked at his face and knew him at once...*

*When I asked why they were selling these poor people he replied, "For money, my child, the price of human blood." His words were subdued and low, as though he wanted no one but me to hear, but I noticed the young mulatto girl caught every word he said and her face lighted up with a strange hope.*

*"What will they do with them, Mr Cope, when they buy them?" I asked, "Take them away to the South and work them like beasts just as we do horses and oxen without pay or reward," he replied, "Some of them are cruelly beaten and mistreated, though this is not often done by the masters, as it is not to their interest to do so. It is ordinarily done by their slave drivers without the knowledge of the owners. They are mere employees who work on a salary and try to make a big showing at the end of the year by increased crops at the physical expense of the slaves in order to retain their positions. One of the worst features of this accursed traffic is the separation of families husband and wife, parent and child, brother and sister. But this is not all my child," here his voice dropped to almost a whisper, "this is not the worst, would to God it were!"*

*"You do not know now, but you will when you are older. Some masters are not content to own the bodies, they are ruining the souls of their female slaves. Oh my boy, God is gathering a swift and terrible judgment to the people who are doing these things. If you live, you will see terrible times for these wrongs. Be a man when it comes."*[17]

---

[17] John Salisbury Cochran. *Bonnie Belmont: A Historical Romance of the Days of Slavery and the Civil War* (1907).

Jeremy T.K. Farley

# Chapter Four

# Virginia's Path to War

In chapter three of this book, we discovered that Western Virginia was supportive to the 'Southern Cause' in its voting and sympathies. In this chapter, we will take a look at the true reasons leaders in the Northern Panhandle of the state desired to break from the Commonwealth in the spring of 1861: SECURITY!

A testament to former Speaker of the House Tip O'Neill's famous quote, "All politics is local," the industrialists and ruling class in Northwestern Virginia were far more concerned about their own personal securities than driven by some type of angelic ideology years ahead of their time.

The election of 1860 was one where slavery was the driving issue. Breckinridge, Douglas and Bell all stood on one side of the issue, with varying degrees of fervency, while Lincoln stood alone on the other end of the spectrum – adamantly opposed to the very institution of itself.

Love him or hate him for it, the tall and lanky senator from Illinois was to the nation the embodiment of abolitionism.

No other election in American history has been defined by such a singular, sectional and significant issue as the Presidential Election of 1860 and though Wheeling, Virginia, was home to a sizable number of zealous abolitionists, the reality is that this crowd represented only a tiny fraction of the electorate of Ohio County – one only needs to see the 1860 election results to confirm this.

With the election being so clearly defined by a single issue, we are able to deduce some very clear realities from its results in the Northern Panhandle.

In Ohio County, a locality most known to harbor abolition sentiments, 3,604 men went to the polls in November 1860. Of those 3,604 men, only 771 of them cast their lot for the most ardent abolitionist on the ballot, whereas 915 of these same residents voted for the outspoken and staunchly pro-slavery candidate John C. Breckinridge – the remaining voters, it seems, were indifferent to either side and simply wanted peace.

Far from being principled in their convictions, the reality is Wheeling and its neighboring communities in the state's northern exclave simply chose the path of least resistance once the bullets began flying, and that path led them directly into the arms of the North.

## Northern West Virginia's Great Fear

Just yards from Ohio to their left and a handful of miles from the Pennsylvania border to their right, local leaders in Wheeling, as well as the rest of the Northern Panhandle, feared – and understandably so – what a war against the North would spell for them personally.

Many times from November 1860 to May 1861 did the people of the Northern Panhandle contemplate what Virginia secession would spell for them as a region.

Merely by glancing at a topographical map, we can see their fears clearly illustrated and can sympathize with their anxieties.

They had no desire to see themselves isolated from the southern states and exposed to the mercies of an invading army from the north. The counties bordering on the Ohio and those drained by the upper waters of the Monongahela were so close to Ohio and Pennsylvania that in the event of war they could be overrun by Federal troops in a few days. The largest city in the section, Wheeling, was only sixty-six miles distant from Pittsburgh. Its large manufacturing interests could be easily destroyed within forty-eight hours of war being declared. Other Ohio River towns occupied positions only a degree less exposed. Troops concentrating at Pittsburgh could penetrate into the very heart of western Virginia simply by going up the Monongahela River.

On April 20, 1861, an article appeared in the *Wheeling Intelligencer* making the case as to why the community should side with the North:

*"We are as powerless as an infant would be in the grasp of Hercules. They could crush us in a day. Cannon planted on the Ohio hills would lay us in ruin. Never did a people occupy a more unenviable position for a hostile collision with their neighbors. Where, in case of collision are we to look for help? From Richmond, away off across the mountains? We might as well look to the moon for help. She will have her hands full and it will keep her busy enough to entertain Jeff Davis's army of occupation. No help there for us. The Secessionists here must remember that Pennsylvania has never yet abandoned her claim to this strip of territory.* (referring to the northern Panhandle, over which Virginia and Pennsylvania had disputed many years) *On the contrary, she has again and again asserted her claim to it. Suppose we were now to set ourselves against the Government. Why, she would have us in a week's time."*

Though these fears were more than realized by Virginia's Northern Panhandle counties, the localities that would become West Virginia's southern and eastern counties did not share these fears.

Unlike the counties of the Ohio and Monongahela river valleys to their north, the West Virginia counties to the south were naturally protected from an invading army – surrounded on all flanks by nearly impenetrable hills. A Yankee army might attempt marching through the Tug Valley, but doing so would require an invading general to take extreme risks for a small prize.

Any invasion of Southern West Virginia would be little more than a Pyrrhic victory for Union forces.

The disparity between the northern and southern sections of West Virginia concerning secession was just beginning to rear its ugly head.

In the days ahead, these southern counties not only took no real part in the formation of the new state of West Virginia, but opposed it as far as they were able.

## Virginia's Secession

In early June 1861, my great-grandfather's grandfather, Thomas Benton Farley, the son of a salt miner from Logan County, Virginia, did what most other young men from his community were doing that month and enlisted to fight in defense of his homeland, the Commonwealth of Virginia.

Three months later, Thomas convinced his brother, William Anderson "Anse" Farley (Pictured below) to enlist as well.

Like most of the stout and formidable men who answered the Old Dominion's call for volunteers, my great-great-great grandfather and his brother did not own slaves, nor were they zealous in fighting for the rights of others to participate in the archaic system – the driving force for them, as well as so many other young men from Western Virginia's southern counties was that their home state was under attack.

The previous December, the State of South Carolina had seceded from the Union following the election of the nation's first Republican president, Abraham Lincoln.

The election of Lincoln, who was outspokenly opposed to the institution of slavery, simply proved to be too much for plantation territories of the Deep South to bear.

South Carolina's withdrawal from the Union was quickly followed by that of Georgia, Florida, Alabama, Mississippi, Louisiana and Texas, all of which had left the Union by February 1, 1861.

Immediately following the November election, Virginia Governor John Letcher called for a special session of the Virginia General Assembly to consider, among other issues, the creation of a secession convention.

Despite the governor's call, the request went unanswered for nearly two months until the General Assembly approved the convention on January 14, 1861.

### February 4, 1861

February 4, 1861, may very well have been the most storied day in American politics. On this date, so many events of historic significance were set to motion that it is almost impossible to know where to begin in explaining them.

First and foremost, it was on this date that leaders from the sovereign states of South Carolina, Mississippi, Florida, Alabama, Georgia, Louisiana and the Republic of Texas met in Montgomery, Alabama, and officially formed the Confederate States of America.

Simultaneously, at the request of the Virginia legislature, a National Peace Conference, led by Virginia's former President of the United States, John Tyler, was held in Washington.

There, inside the District of Columbia's Willard's Hotel, more than 100 leading politicians from across the nation gathered in a futile attempt to orchestrate a compromise between the southern states that had yet to secede from the Union and their northern counterparts. The meeting would continue through most of the month of February 1861.

Serving as the nation's most influential border state with territory reaching farther north than portions of Long Island, Virginia's Richmond government can be complimented for its slow to action approach in the face of a local citizenry in Richmond hungry for secession and war with Mr. Lincoln.

Also on this same date, Virginians again went to the polls, 145,700 in all, electing, by county, 152 representatives who would serve in a statewide convention that would determine whether the state should or should not secede from the Union to which it had been joined for the past eighty-five years.

Thirty of these elected delegates were strict secessionists, thirty were firm unionists and ninety-two were moderates who were not clearly identified with either side and remained undetermined.

Though there were many Virginia politicians calling for immediate secession, at this point they were clearly outnumbered.

## Virginia's Secession Convention

The 152 representatives elected on February 4, 1861, gathered at the Richmond Mechanics Institute on February 13.

One of the convention's first actions was to create a 21 member Federal Relations Committee tasked with reaching a compromise to the sectional differences as they affected Virginia. The committee was comprised of 4 secessionists, 10 moderates and 7 unionists.

Initially, there was no urgency to the convention's deliberations, as all sides felt that time only aided their cause.

Additionally, there were great hopes that the National Peace Conference gathered in Washington might resolve the crisis.

Unfortunately, in the days ahead, the National Peace Conference would prove ineffective and result in near total failure.

With the peace conference in the nation's capital city disintegrating, many of the more moderate delegates began to waver, one-by-one siding with the secessionists.

The deciding factor, however, would come on the afternoon of March 4, 1861.

It was on this date that Senator Abraham Lincoln would address the nation for the first time as President Abraham Lincoln, in his inaugural address.

Critics chided the newly elected President's tone, saying that his speech was "argumentative" and "defiant."

Robertson quotes an observer of the speech saying, "Mr. Lincoln raised his voice and distinctly emphasized the declaration that he must take, 'hold, possess, and occupy the property and places [in the South] belonging to the United States.' This was unmistakable, and he paused for a moment after closing the sentence as if to allow it to be fully taken in and comprehended by his audience."[18]

In the days following Lincoln's speech, rallies were held throughout the Commonwealth, demanding Virginia's legislators secede from the Union at once and join their "Southern Brethren" immediately.

Sensing a growing tide of rebellion, secessionist Lewis Edwin Harvie of Amelia County called for a vote for immediate secession from the Union on April 4, 1861, still, a testament to the Virginia General Assembly's cautiousness and reluctance to go to war, the resolution was voted down 88 to 45.

## Lincoln's Federal Draft

Though the President did not initially outright reject South Carolina's sovereignty or right to secede, the Lincoln Administration refused to abandon American naval forts and military bases located throughout the south, arguing that the bases were property of the Federal government and that they would be defended to the utmost, warning, "if ... an unprovoked assault has been made upon Fort Sumter, I shall hold myself at liberty to re-possess, if I can, like places which have been seized before the Government was devolved upon me."

Lincoln's determination was especially grievous to the pro-Unionist majority serving in the Virginia legislature, who feared being caught in the middle of a battle between Lincoln and their fellow southerners.

As the nation edged closer to Civil War, the convention narrowly voted 63-57 to send a three man delegation to Washington to determine from Lincoln what his intentions were regarding the seceded states.

In what can only be seen as 'Divine Interference,' the ambassadors dispatched to Washington to meet with Lincoln were delayed several days due to inclement weather.

They had hoped to be successful in brokering a peace between the seceding states and the newly sworn-in President.

Unfortunately, the delegation arrived in Washington on April 12, just as Confederate forces had initiated their were bombardment of

---

[18] Robertson p. 8. Robertson

the Federal government's military base at Fort Sumter, South Carolina, ushering in what would become America's bloodiest war.

Who knows if this Virginia delegation could have brokered a peace and avoided the tragic American Civil War. One thing that is known, however, is that once the first cannons were fired, any hope for a peaceful conclusion to the hostilities were ended.

President Lincoln advised the group of Virginians of his intent to hold the fort and respond to force with force.

In Richmond, large public demonstrations in support of the Confederacy were held and all hope for Virginia to remain in the Union, serving as mediator between the Deep South and Washington was quickly vanishing.

Within a matter of days, President Abraham Lincoln issued a call to all states that had not declared secession, including Virginia, for troops to assist in halting the insurrection and recover the captured federal forts in what was now the Confederate States of America.

The U.S. Secretary of War, Simon Cameron, issued the following letter to the Governor of Virginia on April 15, 1861:

*To His Excellency the Governor of Virginia:*

*Sir: Under the act of Congress for calling forth 'militia to execute the laws of the Union, suppress insurrections, repel invasions, etc.,' approved February 28, 1795, I have the honor to request your Excellency to cause to be immediately detached from the militia of your State the quota designated in the table below, to serve as infantry or rifleman for the period of three months, unless sooner discharged.*

*Your Excellency will please communicate to me the time, at or about, which your quota will be expected at its rendezvous, as it will be met as soon as practicable by an officer to muster it into the service and pay of the United States.*

*— Simon Cameron, Secretary of War.*

Cameron's quota for Virginia called for three regiments of 2,340 men to rendezvous at Staunton, Wheeling and Gordonsville.

With the Old Dominion hanging in the balance, even leaning toward the Union, despite the local war-hawk population gathered at Richmond, Secretary Cameron's call for Virginians to wage a bloody war against their friends and neighbors to their south proved to be the final straw.

Governor Letcher considered Lincoln's request "for troops to invade and coerce" to be lacking in constitutional authority, and out of scope with the Congressional Act of 1795.

The Virginia governor issued the following reply to the nation's Department of War:

*Sir: I have received your telegram of the 15th, the genuineness of which I doubted. Since that time I have received your communications mailed the same day, in which I am requested to detach from the militia of the State of Virginia 'the quota assigned in a table,' which you append, 'to serve as infantry or rifleman for the period of three months, unless sooner discharged.'*

*In reply to this communication, I have only to say that the militia of Virginia will not be furnished to the powers at Washington for any such use or purpose as they have in view. Your object is to subjugate the Southern States, and a requisition made upon me for such an object - an object, in my judgment, not within the purview of the Constitution or the act of 1795 - will not be complied with. You have chosen to inaugurate civil war, and, having done so, we will meet it in a spirit as determined as the administration has exhibited toward the South.*

*— Respectfully, John Letcher*

Lincoln's desire to call Virginia's bluff and force her into a civil war allied with the Union would prove to be the tipping point for the undecided legislators.

"Virginia's Unionists could tolerate the insult the Republicans represented; when the federal government rejected that sovereignty, the threat could no longer be denied even by those who loved the

Union," wrote American historian and former president of the University of Richmond Edward L. Ayers.[19]

Virginia could no longer tolerate the insult the new Republican Administration posed to the Commonwealth's sovereignty. The President's demand for the blood of Virginia's youth to be shed in a war against the Carolinas and Georgia was simply too much for the State's leaders to tolerate or condone.

Once Lincoln made his demand for Virginia's soldiers, the Old Dominion's destiny was forever sealed, she was a southern state and she would fight in defense of the South.

Following Governor Letcher's letter, the secession convention voted on April 17, provisionally, to secede, on the condition of ratification by a statewide referendum.

The final vote of the secession convention was 88 to 55, with delegates representing the following West Virginia counties requesting to be listed as having voted for the secession ordinance:

Barbour, Boone, Calhoun, Gilmer, Logan, Wyoming, McDowell, Fayette, Raleigh, Hardy, Jackson, Roane, Mercer, Monroe, Morgan, Pocahontas, Ritchie, Upshur, Wetzel and Wirt.

As the above map of West Virginia reveals, the

Map of West Virginia counties whose delegates voted in favor of secession (in black).
*NOTE: The counties of Berkely and Jefferson were not initially part of the Mountain State.

decision to remain loyal to the North was hardly universal in what would become West Virginia, especially among that region's duly elected officials.

"It is a peculiar fact," writes James McGregor, " that across the mountains in West Virginia a majority of those counties which

---

[19] E.L. Ayers, p. 141.

Congress later recognized as Union counties were placed by their representatives in the secession column."

After the passage of the ordinance, the pace with which events began to move quickly escalated.

$100,000 was appropriated for the defense of the state.

An act was passed suspending the authority of the Federal Government until the ratification of the secession ordinance.

Another act authorized the Governor to inform President Jefferson Davis of Virginia's desire to enter the Confederacy.

If Virginia blood was to be shed in an American Civil War, the Commonwealth's leaders desired it to be in defense of Dixie rather than in an alliance with Massachusetts and Ohio.

A proclamation was issued ordering all volunteer companies in the state to prepare for immediate action.

The following day, the arsenal at Harper's Ferry was captured and most of the machinery was moved to Richmond.

Union forces stationed at the naval yard at Norfolk began torching their own ships and destroying Naval facilities fearing a similar seizure of American property.

Virginia had entered the American Civil War on the side of the South... and so had at least twenty-one counties of West Virginia.

Chapter
Five

# The First
# Wheeling Convention

Though the secession vote of April 17, 1861, was merely to authorize a statewide referendum which would determine whether or not the Old Dominion would divorce itself from the United States, leaders in Richmond wasted no time in preparing to be a sovereign state.

The statewide popular vote confirming secession was seen by politicians in Richmond as nothing more than a necessary formality — and for good reason, the general sentiments held throughout the state by the common man (including much of western Virginia) was to leave the Union.

In the public's mind, their elected officials had taken far too long in joining the Southern Cause.

In the eyes of the average 19th century Virginia citizen, a fanatical presidential candidate who had only received 1.2% of their state's votes had been elected president and the time had come to break all allegiances with the nation he now commanded.

At any rate, when the day should come for the vote of the people, Virginia would be engaged in war and it mattered little whether the electorate approved or rejected the ordinance.

The convention adjourned on Wednesday, May 1, 1861, with delegates of the secession convention returning to their districts as the state prepared itself for a military conflict against the very flag it had claimed as its own for nearly a century.

In the hours following the April 17th Virginia Secession Convention's decision to put secession to a vote before the voters of the Commonwealth, a handful of representatives from northwestern Virginia met secretly inside the hotel room of Wheeling delegate Sherrard Clemens.

### Sherrard Clemens

Born in Wheeling, Virginia, Clemens received an appointment to the United States Military Academy in West Point, New York, but resigned after only six months.

PORTRAIT: Sherrard Clemens

Instead, Clemens opted to attend Washington College in Washington, Pennsylvania, and was admitted to the bar in 1843, commencing practice in Wheeling. He was first elected to the United States House of Representatives in 1852 and then reelected, serving again from 1857 to 1861.

Throughout the Secession Convention, Clemens irked southern sympathizers with his intense loyalty to the North and perceived unwillingness to compromise on any issue.

Sometime during this same year, O. Jennings Wise, son of Virginia's former Governor and staunch Southerner, challenged Clemens to a duel over words the Wheeling attorney had used against the South.

Engaged to marry a woman later that year, Clemens refused to give in to Wise's demands for a duel.

Back in Wheeling, Clemens' fiancé heard that her espoused husband had refused to face Wise in a duel and sent him word that she would not marry him until he fought his Southern agitator.

The July 22, 1888, edition of the *Atlanta Constitution* concludes its narrative of the story with, "He did fight, and Wise's shot lamed him for life."

Practicing a discretion that is entirely unknown by today's media, the 19th century newspaper article failed to provide the full and far more entertaining details of this incident.

The son of Virginia's southern governor shot the northern Congressman in his right testicle.

Undeterred by her husband—elect's injuries, Clemens' fiancé remained true to her word, marrying the Congressman later this same year… despite his humiliating injuries!

## A Secret Meeting is Held

While inside Sherrard's room at the Powhatan Hotel in Downtown Richmond, a handful of the delegates from Northwestern Virginia, realizing that the voters of the Commonwealth would overwhelmingly favor secession, determined to return to their districts early and begin rallying the people against leaving the Union.

Though they could not expect to defeat secession by vote, a series of loyalist town hall meetings held throughout northwestern Virginia, they hoped, would signal a false message to the Lincoln Administration that the vast-majority of citizens of Western Virginia were strong supporters of the Union cause, even if their government in Richmond was not.

*Lincoln Stepped Too Far*

As the plotting delegates returned to their homes in Western Virginia and began hosting a series of local meetings, two things became grossly clear to the men who had gathered secretly inside the hotel room of Congressman Clemens:

1.) The people of Western Virginia did not want war

2.) The people of Western Virginia felt as though the Lincoln Administration was the primary driving force for military hostilities.

Rather than prove their loyalty to the North, as was wished for by the meetings' organizers, the series of northwestern meetings actually had the opposite effect.

Most of the community assemblies held throughout the northern region of what would become the Mountain State often dissolved into uncontrollable outbursts by those in attendance, ranting against the actions of the Washington authorities.

Several Northwestern Virginia newspapers recorded these events, quoting citizens who asserted that Lincoln was more desirous for bloodletting than the war-hawks in Richmond.

In particular, residents of nearly every northwestern county were especially disapproving of Lincoln's call for Virginia troops to assist in putting down a rebellion in South Carolina.

An editor of one of the western papers supporting the Union wrote that he had traveled all over Western Virginia, and while the people generally did not see any reason for Virginia's secession, "at the same time they were far from approving Lincoln's course."

The April 25, 1861, edition of *The Parkersburg Gazette* went even further in its criticism of the Lincoln Administration's demand for Western Virginia soldiers to fight against rebels in South Carolina:

"...the people of northwestern Virginia, heretofore honest Union men, after the exposure of the treachery of Lincoln will indignantly repudiate Unionism. No people are more patriotic than ours but when 'Black Republicanism' looks for encouragement and support in its crusade against the South it will look in vain in West Virginia."

Though harsh in its words, the northern West Virginia newspaper article further backs the conclusions drawn from the election results of November 1860: though many in Northwestern Virginia were not enthusiastic supporters of secession, they were even less passionate in joining the Union fight.

Their true desire was simply to be left alone.

## Wheeling is Selected

Undeterred by a series of town hall meetings that can be described as producing mixed results at best, John S. Carlile, a loyalist delegate from Harrison County, issued a declaration that the loyal citizens of West Virginia should come together in order to "secure their position in the Union."

Rather than choose a central location for delegates to meet, Carlile and other loyalists demanded instead that the convention be held in Wheeling, in the state's extreme northwestern exclave.

PHOTO: John Carlile
U.S. Library of Congress

Geographically positioned farther north than the City of Philadelphia, Wheeling, which was roughly a +300 mile journey from the state's southern counties such as Logan, Mercer and Monroe was selected simply because it was the only city in Western Virginia where there was hope of finding a Union majority. To have had the meeting elsewhere would have invited opportunities for secessionist majorities.

Had Parkersburg, Clarksburg, Fairmont or even Morgantown been nearly as loyal as they have usually been considered, these locations would have undoubtedly been chosen over Wheeling due to their more geographically central locations; however, those places were not selected and the State of West Virginia had its birth in a distant and narrow peninsula, far removed from the rest of the state.

Due to this reality, it is impossible to separate the history of West Virginia from the history of Wheeling.

Here was published Virginia's one paper which took up the anti-slavery cause, *The Wheeling Intelligencer*, consistently urging for the division of the state and supported the Republican administration in its efforts to put down the rebellion.

With its local, state, and national officials generally favorable to the Union, with nearly one-third of its population foreign-born and altogether out of sympathy with the Southern Cause, and with its proximity to Ohio and Pennsylvania, Wheeling logically became the soul of the "new state movement." As such, it was recognized throughout the North and the new government was commonly referred to as "the Wheeling government."

## A People Aren't Notified

One would think that a call for something as important as creating an entirely new state, as well as officially switching national allegiances from the one to which their state government had legally sworn (Confederate States of America), would be immediately followed by a vast information campaign aimed at notifying as many local officials and citizens in the localities up for grabs as possible – or at least we can all agree that doing this would have been the right thing to do.

Despite the magnitude of their proposal, we find that in the First Wheeling Convention no fewer than two-thirds of the counties now constituting the State of West Virginia were either never notified or showed no desire to take part in these meetings.

Nevertheless, the self-appointed "representatives" of the First Wheeling Convention set events in motion which would ultimately change the lives of millions of individuals, as well as create one of the poorest and most oppressed states in American history.

### *Those who were notified were not pleased*

Clarksburg, in Harrison County, was the home of John S. Carlile, who was successful in convincing many of the town's most prominent citizens to join the new state movement, however, these sentiments seemed to have vanished once one left the town limits, as the rest of the county was "over run with Southern sympathizers."

Union men meeting in Wheeling often complained that they were being subjected to all kinds of annoyance by their neighbors. One man writes that he hopes the report is true that a company of Secessionists was being raised in his district to join the war effort, for the county would then be relieved of "a large amount of the off scouring of humanity."[20]

## Choosing the "Representatives"

The delegates to the first Wheeling Convention were chosen in such an irregular manner that a description of the methods by which they were chosen has never been discovered.

In the larger towns informal mass meetings were held and representatives elected. The rural districts, where three-fourths of the people resided, had no opportunity to take part in the movement and most of the residents of these communities were unaware that any organized effort was even being made to neutralize the effect of the ordinance of secession. Since the convention was not called by any authority recognized by the state constitution, each county was a law unto itself.

The feeling prevailed that the more delegates present, the more impressive the effect would be, not so much in West Virginia as throughout the North. Thus the four hundred and twenty-nine men who assembled in Wheeling on May 13, 1861, made an impressive showing and deceived the newspaper correspondents as to the real situation in the interior of the state.

The counties represented at the first Wheeling Convention were: Hancock, Brooke, Ohio, Marshall, Marion, Monongalia, Preston, Harrison, Wood, Ritchie, Lewis, Upshur, Gilmer, Wirt, Jackson, Mason, Wetzel, Pleasants, Barbour, Hampshire, Berkeley, Taylor, Tyler, Doddridge and Roane.

A closer analysis shows that more than one-third of the total number of delegates were from the communities immediately surrounding Wheeling.

Hancock County, West Virginia's northernmost county, with a total population of 4,445, was represented by thirty-two delegates (1 delegate per 138 residents); Brooke County, slightly larger than Hancock, sent sixteen; Marshall County, with a population of 12,997,

---

[20] Granville Davisson Hall. *The Rending of Virginia* (1902), p. 218-219.

71

sent seventy men as her quota. As a general rule, the farther the county was away from the City of Wheeling, the fewer number of delegates they had representing them at the Wheeling Convention.

Far from being a convention of Western Virginia counties, the assembly gathered at Wheeling was merely a regional meeting of political leaders, office seekers, curiosity seekers and rabble rousers.

In essence, the First Wheeling Convention, which began on May 13, 1861, was nothing more than a poorly advertised, self-appointed assembly without any more of a legal right to make lawful decisions, pass acts or issue decrees than a political rally gathered anywhere else in the state.

The convention failed to include a single representative from twenty-six counties that would eventually be brought under their control – a violation of the most basic universal human right of self-determination. These unrepresented localities include the counties of Boone, Braxton, Cabell, Calhoun, Clay, Fayette, Gilmer, Greenbrier, Hardy, Jefferson, Kanawha, Logan (including modern-day Mingo), McDowell, Mercer, Monroe, Morgan, Nicholas, Pendleton, Pocahontas, Putnam, Raleigh, Randolph, Tucker, Wayne, Webster and Wyoming – it should be noted that in the years ahead, many of these very same localities would be underrepresented in the newly created state's legislature, suffering unequal treatment when it came to capital improvement projects, education and worker's rights.

In the decades that followed the Civil War, residents of these southern counties would become the object of scorn to the elitists in the northern ruling class.

Given the indignities the strong and hardworking people of McDowell, Mingo or any other southern county have suffered over the past century and a half, it would be hard to make a case that the residents of these localities have fared any better under the western government than had they been permitted to continue with the government in Richmond; which was what they clearly desired at the outbreak of the American Civil War.

Instead, these prizes of war – all of which were overwhelmingly loyal to the South – would be viewed in the years to come almost as a distant colony, filled with less-than-human laborers; a workforce that would suffer the chains of enslavement throughout the opening half of the state's tempestuous history, only to spend the more recent days searching for work and broken by heavy drug use, neglect and joblessness.

In West Virginia's first seventy-five years or existence, industrialists from outside the state would terrorize the people of these overlooked counties – under the full blessing and protection of the newly created state's highest-ranking government officials. These wealthy tycoons, mined the fruits of the land and then vanished away, leaving only empty holes in their wake.

## May 13, 1861 – First Wheeling Convention

Records from the three-day meeting reveal that even the organizers of the convention were in disagreement pertaining to their legal rights as an assembly as well as the ultimate purpose of their meeting.

John Jay Jackson, Jr., of Wood County, a man whom biographers described as having a "refreshing frankness" stated that he did not believe the assembly to be anything more than "a large and imposing mass meeting, called irregularly and informally for the purpose of consulting the United States authorities as to the best means of procedure."

On the other hand, the ambitious Winchester-born attorney, John S. Carlile, who represented Harrison County, considered the convention to be "a sovereign body and as such could do anything the sovereign people could do."

In the opening moments of debate, Jackson expressed his opinion that they had come together to deliberate, "not to form a new state."

Carlile retorted that if he had so understood the purpose of the meeting he would have stayed at home. The people, he said, expected them to remain in session until their safety was secured beyond a doubt; but "if we temporize now and consult and adjourn to come back here again, before that day arrives you will have sworn allegiance to the rattlesnake flag."

On this same day, those in attendance of the Wheeling Convention elected Dr. John Moss of Wood County to serve as the convention's president.

Within an hour's time, Jackson again took to the floor, requesting that the convention be adjourned "until a more thorough canvass of the counties could be made."

The Wood County attorney did not believe that the convention properly represented the people of Western Virginia and, if it acted at all, would act without their consent. The interior counties, he said, had not shown the slightest desire or inclination to enter into the movement.

Carlile answered that only prompt action could save them now. The Federal Government should be called upon for aid, which would be furnished only if their measures were decisive. "Let us repudiate these monstrous usurpations; let us show our loyalty to Virginia and the Union; and let us maintain ourselves in the Union at every hazard. It is useless to cry peace when there is no peace."

## May 14, 1861 – First Wheeling Convention

The second day of the First Wheeling Convention began with a delegate from Ohio County introducing a series of resolutions.

Among the resolutions introduced by the Wheeling representative were bills which declared:

1.) The ordinance of secession to be null and void
2.) The prohibition of the election of representatives to Congress was a usurpation of power
3.) That the action of putting the military power of the state in the hands of the seceding states was a violation of the constitution
4.) That all citizens were urged to vote against the ordinance of secession.

Carlile, who objected on principle to all resolutions but his own, came forward with a proposition to sever at once the Tenth and Eleventh Congressional Districts, with the addition of Wayne County, from the rest of Virginia and to form a free and independent state in the Union.

He would have a committee appointed to draw up a constitution for the new state which should be called New Virginia.

Carlile's motion was met by a storm of protest from representatives at the convention, many of whom were taken aback at the thought of forming a new state so quickly and with so little deliberation.

Mr. George K. Wheat, the Ohio County delegate who introduced the initial four resolutions, protested that Carlile was going too fast even for him.

John Jay Jackson declared that if any proposition regarding the creation of a new state was given serious consideration, he would go home and take the entire Wood County delegation with him.

Carlile denied that the action proposed was either hasty or revolutionary, but asserted that it was the only alternative left if the people declined to abide by the action of the Richmond Convention.

After harsh debate which lasted for several hours, the convention went into recess, set to reconvene the following day.

## May 15, 1861 – First Wheeling Convention

The Ides of May brought resumed debate as the level of tension inside the three–story Custom House for the Western District of Virginia, known today as West Virginia Independence Hall, reached an even greater height.

As Carlile continued to pressure delegates into creating "New Virginia," things inside the Wheeling assembly hall reached a boiling point.

Waitman T. Willey, a Morgantown representative and staunch Republican, interrupted Carlile, the Harrison County representative, stating that the idea of creating a new state was nothing less than "treason against the state government, the government of the United States and the government of the Confederate States of America."

PHOTO: West Virginia Independence Hall, located in downtown Wheeling. Built in 1859 as a federal custom house and courthouse, it soon served as West Virginia's state capitol during the American Civil War *(Public Domain)*

## Willey's Slip-Up, Recognizing the C.S.A.

Willey's statement is noteworthy in that it recognized the Confederate States of America as a sovereign nation.

Perhaps even more striking is the fact that out of the hundreds of "representatives" meeting at the convention, not a single person stood to repudiate his remark.

If the Confederacy had a legal existence, the Wheeling Convention and government certainly did not – the Wheeling Convention was founded on the assumption that states could not legally secede from the Union.

Granting that Virginia's action in uniting with the Southern Confederacy was legal, then the whole movement in Wheeling must be considered as outright treason.

Following this exchange, it was suggested that the convention go into secret session; however, after taking a vote it was determined that the convention should remain in open session.

After the vote, Carlile modified his original proposition to provide for the calling of a convention in June, in the event of the voters ratifying the ordinance of secession in the upcoming mid-May statewide vote.

The convention adjourned that evening after having agreed to meet back on June 11, this would allow time for Virginia to officially secede from the United States (The voters had not yet gone to the polls to ratify the ordinance of secession, though there was little doubt that the people of the Commonwealth would do just that).

It was also agreed that upon returning, the assembly be better organized. It was suggested that each invited county be entitled to twice as many delegates as it had representatives in the House of Delegates.

By and large, the May 1861 meeting of union loyalists was an utter failure. Not only had they failed to present a unified front to the Lincoln Administration, but the hopes of men such as Francis H. Pierpont and John Carlile, who fully anticipated leaving the convention with a constitution for the State of New Virginia, had been mercilessly destroyed.

There were, even in northwestern Virginia, very few individuals interested in forming a new state and warring against the motherland.

Even the newspaper reporters from across the nation who had descended upon the Ohio River community were forced to recognize the inconvenient fact that northern loyalty among the Western

Virginia counties was significantly less than what they had been led to believe.

Possibly the best commentaries on the May 1861 convention are to be found in the *Pittsburgh Chronicle*.

On his first day in Wheeling, a Pittsburgh reporter wrote that northwestern Virginia was "as loyal to the Union as Pennsylvania herself."

Only forty-eight hours later, the correspondent writes back that he was convinced that the Union element was far from being as strong as had been initially reported.

There were a great many in Wheeling who were going to follow the state out of the Union, and while these people were not making much noise, their opposition to the Union cause was felt none the less plainly.

Out of eleven militia companies in Wheeling, the United States recruiting officer had been able to persuade only two men to enlist and these refused to leave the city.

In the convention itself, the greatest difference of opinion could be observed. The advocates for the new state included a number of the most prominent men, but the vast majority of the delegates were opposed to the division of Virginia, as was the common man.

The men gathered in Wheeling could not agree on any course of action and the bitterest jealousies were cropping out each day – northern people who were following the convention in the newspapers were being deceived, declared one writer.

They did not know that on the evening of the 13th of May a meeting of citizens and delegates was held where it was urged that West Virginia should stand neutral in the coming conflict, as the North could not expect West Virginians to slaughter their Virginia brethren. "With such feeling existing," remarks the correspondent, "it could scarcely be the duty of the Federal Government to protect this section from the Secessionists, and unless there was a sudden change of heart, the fate of West Virginia was sealed and the country would be overrun with Union troops."[21]

---

[21] *Pittsburgh Chronicle*, May 16, 1861.

## Northern Media Commentary

The adjournment of the convention without taking decisive measures to ensure West Virginia's place in the Union was the source of much dissatisfaction in the North.

Members of the media who served as the Lincoln Administration's lapdogs agreed that a more disappointing gathering could scarcely have been held.

It was a common criticism that a disproportionate amount of time had been spent in making speeches; even the most loyal of the delegates seemed to be willing to give little more than lip service to the Union cause.

Moreover, it was a colossal shock to those who had been informed that the Western Virginians were loyal to Lincoln only to discover that this loyalty was inspired by the fear of what would happen to them in case they submitted to the legislation of the state authorities at Richmond.

There were many allusions to "hanging" and delegates at the convention did not attempt to hide their fear of being caught in the middle of a war between their state government and the full weight of an invading Federal army situated just yards across the river.

Even in the North, newspapers and media outlets could not reach an agreement on the best course of action residents of the western counties should pursue.

Conservative papers agreed that the United States Constitution could not be stretched enough to allow a new state to be formed in Virginia.

Besides, the loyalty of Virginia's western region was far from assured, as the presence of Secessionists in the convention showed.

The feeling which did exist in West Virginia favoring the division of the state was inspired not by love of the Union, but by the remembrance of old sectional differences or by opportunistic politicians seeking higher office.

Even the Lincoln government initially held severe reservations about dissecting an entirely new state out of the Old Dominion – breaking apart Virginia at this time would be a tacit recognition of the actual secession of the Southern state and this was exactly what the Federal government wished to avoid.

So long as Virginia was officially recognized as still being a state of the Federal Union, her legislature must be the only legislature that could be recognized under the Constitution. "A legislative body could not commit treason, although its members might," they argued.

If the legislature of Virginia in session at Richmond could be induced to give its consent to the separation of the western counties, everything would be regular and constitutional. But until that extraordinarily improbable event occurred, there was no way by which New Virginia could have anything but a provisional government of her own.

Jeremy T.K. Farley

# Chapter Six

# The Second Wheeling Convention

Still licking their wounds from the three-day May convention, northwestern Virginia politicians pushing for the creation of a new state embarked upon what can best be described as the greatest public relations campaign in Western Virginia's history.

Addresses written by Carlile and other leaders were scattered throughout the northwestern counties of Virginia, decrying Virginia secession and begging local citizens to stand true to the federal government.

Carlile and his cohorts set out to rally their base, while at the same time not draw too much ire from the majority of citizens who desired neither the division of their country nor of their state.

It is significant to observe that the question of separating from Virginia was not even hinted at during this time of campaigning, instead, Carlile denounced the actions of the Richmond Secessionists, urging the "loyal people" to "repudiate their treasonable proceedings."

Early commentaries about Carlile state, "[he] had evidently learned a lesson in the meeting which had just closed. Never again did he heartily espouse the cause."[22]

Instead, the state that would become West Virginia would be formed behind closed doors and without the knowledge or consent of the common people – or for that matter, many of their elected representatives.

## West Virginia Votes

On Thursday, May 23, 1861, the ordinance of secession was put to a vote before the people of the Commonwealth of Virginia.

From Wheeling to Wytheville, Charleston to Chesapeake and all points in between, the voters of the Old Dominion set out to their local county polling place and one by one voiced their opinion regarding whether the Commonwealth should secede from the Union.

In some eastern and southern counties the vote for secession was unanimous. In southwestern Virginia, the County of Wythe, which at the time bordered what is now West Virginia, voted in favor of secession by a margin of 1,168 to 1. Just across the county line in Mercer County, 93% of the voters there elected to side with the Confederacy.

Farther north, however, the number of counties for and against secession was nearly evenly divided.

The bulk support for the southern cause in what is now West Virginia came from the counties situated along the Alleghany Mountain ridges or those in the southern region.

| County | Votes for secession | Votes against secession |
|--------|---------------------|-------------------------|
| Logan | 518 | 63 |
| McDowell | 196 | 17 |
| Mercer | 871 | 67 |
| Monroe | 1,189 | 79 |
| Greenbrier | 1,016 | 110 |

[22] James C. McGregor.

On the other hand, the most vocal opposition to secession naturally came from the counties bordering Union territory – this should come as no surprise, as a war between the states would create a situation where they would have the most to lose and the least to gain.

| County | Votes for secession | Votes against secession |
| --- | --- | --- |
| Cabell | 232 | 882 |
| Kanawha | 520 | 1,697 |
| *Marshall | 142 | 1,993 |
| Mason | 119 | 1,841 |
| *Ohio | 157 | 3,368 |
| *Hancock | 23 | 743 |
| *Brooke | 109 | 721 |

*Indicates county is located in the Northwestern Panhandle*

The greatest percentages of pro-union votes came from the Northern Panhandle, where counties bordered not one, but two Union states and faced extreme peril in the event of a war as they were bounded by Ohio and Pennsylvania to their west and east.

In total, the counties that made up what would soon become the "Mountain State" were nearly evenly divided in their loyalties at the time of the May 1861 vote as twenty-four counties chose secession and twenty-six opted to remain with the Union – only 52% of West Virginia's counties voted in favor of continuing in the Federal government.

When examining the numbers, it is also important to keep in mind that this vote was simply to determine whether or not Virginia should remain in the Union – it had nothing to do with whether the state should fight for or against the Confederacy.

As was illustrated in the previously shared account of recruiters in Wheeling only being able to successfully recruit two soldiers and event these individuals refused to leave the city limits, most West Virginians from the northern region simply did not want to fight in the Civil War – neither for or against the Union.

### *Clay County: Western Virginia's Most Divided County*

In the spring of 1861, Western Virginia was a divided land and no place was more divided than its central most county of Clay.

There, on May 23, 1861, 204 voters went out to vote concerning secession. 102 voiced their support for remaining in the Union and 102 voted to join the Confederacy.

In western Virginia, the American Civil War would not be waged between forces from South Carolina pitted against those of Massachusetts. Instead, the war would be fought between men from Logan County and those of Brooke County. The days ahead would pit neighbor against neighbor, county against county and brother against brother.

While leaders in the North were struggling to keep a country together, leaders in Richmond were fraught with holding their state together.

## Map of May 23, 1861 Secession Vote

To the right is a map detailing how the residents of West Virginia's counties voted on May 23, 1861. (White – counties whose citizens voted against secession; Gray – counties whose citizens voted for secession.)

## Western Virginia: Invaded by the North & the South

Recognizing that the territory of Western Virginia was up for grabs, both the Northern and Southern governments dispatched troops into the mountains – attempting to sure up support in the region as the continent stood at the doorstep of civil war.

The Confederates were on the ground first, but their companies were comprised mainly of native Virginians.

Grafton was held for several days by a Confederate force and all the country to the south was overrun by Southern troops in a matter of days; interestingly, most of the southern troops were locals.

# The Second Wheeling Convention

The contest over the occupation of West Virginia had barely begun on June 11, 1861, the scheduled date for the Wheeling Convention to meet once again – following the voter's secession from the Union.

On this afternoon, eighty-two men arrived in Wheeling, declaring themselves "representatives of the people."

## An Unelected Body

Of these eighty-two men, only twenty-seven counties were represented – twenty-three of West Virginia's counties either rejected to recognize the convention's legitimacy and refused to send a delegation or outright not invited.

Only 30% of the 'representatives' who filed into the newly constructed custom house for the Western District of Virginia had been elected to serve as a state senator or representative in the Virginia House of Delegates. The remaining 70% came bringing other credentials, ranging from claims of having been selected by county officials to merely being a friend to the cause.

In reality, how the delegates were selected remains a mystery. "It is certain that in many cases not even the form of an election was gone through with. No one believes that the people of Alexandria or of Fairfax County held an open election for representatives to a Union convention. The documents submitted to the committee on credentials would make interesting reading if they could be found. Who conducted the election? In the extreme northwestern counties the county officials attested to the genuineness of the election, but we know that in the great majority of cases the local officers were supporters of the regular state government and would not endorse any revolutionary proceeding like the Wheeling conventions," wrote McGregor.

Of the twenty-three counties which were represented in the Second Wheeling Convention, many of the "representatives" of these localities were there without any blessing or official act from the locally elected officials of their own communities – they simply showed up and claimed to be the representative of these places.

A number of speakers in the convention bore witness to the fact that the civil officials of the counties they represented were secessionists "almost to a man."

One representative from Randolph County declared that "before the advance of the Union troops nearly every judge of our courts, nearly every prosecuting attorney, many of the justices of the peace, the majority of our sheriffs, many of the commissioners of the revenue, and all classes and grades of civil officers had fled to Richmond."

James G. West of Wetzel County (a northern West Virginia county that actually bordered the Mason-Dixon Line) admitted that in his county, "all the officers were secessionists."

Despite acknowledging the reality that the majority of elected officials in the county governments they represented opposed any effort to undermine the state government in Richmond, the men who gathered in Wheeling unashamedly pressed forward with their agenda – deceiving the nation of the true feelings of the local people in their hometowns.

## An Underrepresented Body

By the time the Second Wheeling Convention assembled in mid-June 1861, the Commonwealth of Virginia, including much of what is now West Virginia, had fully embraced the Southern Confederacy and was in the midst of establishing the young nation's capital in Richmond – just 100 miles south of the embattled infant country's northern border.

The recognized and sovereign Virginia government was at this point just as much a part of the Confederacy as the State of South Carolina or that of Alabama.

With only 27 of Virginia's 147 counties "represented" at the June assembly in Wheeling (and of that number, +70% had not even been elected by the people in a legal election), the convention faced a true dilemma: What should they do? What legal power did they have to do anything?

Despite their confusion and uncertainty regarding what they should or even legally could do, the convention was quick to agree on one item – they would not create a new state.

Creating a new state out of Western Virginia, would be a gross usurpation of the people's will – though many Virginians opposed secession, including Robert E. Lee, the comomn attitude was that Virginia was home and any held loyalty would be offered to the Commonwealth… regardless of what national banner flew over her capital.

Even the *Wheeling Intelligencer* was initially opposed to forming a new state, declaring that too many counties were "overrun by secessionists."

If was the goal of Federal authorities was to restore every state government to what it had been prior to the outbreak of war, then dissecting Virginia did not fall within these objectives stated by the Lincoln Administration.

## Corrupt Politics in West Virginia is Birthed

Upon determining that the creation of a new state would be unconstitutional, inflammatory to the South and against the will of the majority of the people who would dwell within the newly created state's borders, the "representatives" in Wheeling declared themselves to be the true and "restored" government of Virginia, proclaiming the sovereign state legislature sitting in Richmond to be null and vacant.

The fact that anyone would even take this group or their declaration serious is laughable considering the fact that fewer than one in five Virginia counties were receiving any type of representation in the assembly and fewer than 30% of the "representatives" seated had actually been legally elected by the people of their districts.

On the other hand, the sitting government in Richmond had been lawfully elected and provided seats and representation for every county and citizen in the entire state – from the Atlantic Ocean to the Ohio River.

The idea of declaring the General Assembly in Richmond vacant and the Wheeling Convention the true and "Restored Government of Virginia" can be traced to the *Wheeling Intelligencer,* who outlined a plan (which was eventually adopted) for the convention to take in order to seize power:

### The proposal included the following points:

- All state offices were to be declared vacant and then filled with only loyal Union men.
- The Federal authorities should be asked to recognize these new officers.
- The convention should remain in session for three or four weeks.
- The members of the convention should be paid out of the funds belonging to the Commonwealth of Virginia.

Throughout its long and turbulent history, West Virginia has been defined by "dirty politics" and a culture of government corruption seems to have permeated itself over the past century.

The dismal record of the Mountain State's elected leaders over the past century should come as no surprise to any student of history: West Virginia's very formation was one of corruption, political trickery and deceit.

Regardless of their intent, the men who gathered inside the three-story building in Wheeling during the summer of 1861 would be forcing the new state down a path of political misconduct which would plague generations to come.

The old 18th century proverb sums up West Virginia's modern-day political misfortunes the best:

### *"As the twig is bent, so grows the tree."*

At a time when West Virginia's government was in its infancy, northern elitists, agenda driven newspapermen and political opportunists descended like vultures upon the mountainous of Western Virginia, usurping the will of the people and creating a state that would be rife with political scandal for centuries to come.

Even today, West Virginia is known throughout the world for its corrupt political machines, an unfortunate distinction for a state whose residents are among the hardest working and most honest inhabitants of the North American continent.

It seems old habits are hard to die – especially when they have been a basic foundation for governing for over 150 years.

"In his best-selling book, *The Making of the President 1960*, Theodore White said that West Virginia was among the most politically corrupt places in the country. The basis for White's observation was the 1960 West Virginia Democratic primary election in which John F. Kennedy buried Hubert Humphrey by a mixture of state-of-the-art political techniques and old-style vote buying.

"There is other evidence to justify White's harsh assessment. In the last third of the 20th century, West Virginia governors were charged with felonies four times in federal court, with two acquittals and two guilty pleas. Two state senate presidents were convicted and sent to prison, and numerous elected and appointed officials (plus a few associates) suffered a similar fate."[23]

The Center of Public Integrity's State Integrity Investigation project recently gave West Virginia an F when it comes to Public Access to Information, State Civil Service Management, Lobbying Disclosure and Redistricting.[24]

## The "Restored Government of Virginia" is Established

The Second Wheeling Convention which met in June named Arthur I. Boreman to serve as its president, Gibson L. Cranmer as secretary and Thomas Hornbrook as sergeant-at-arms.

Following selection of its officers, all members were required to take an oath to "support the Constitution of the United States and the laws made in pursuance thereof as the supreme law of the land, anything in the ordinances of the convention which assembled in Richmond on the 13th of February last to the contrary notwithstanding."

Requiring such an oath ensured that rather than truly serve as an assembly of the people, the Wheeling Convention would be nothing more than a kangaroo court in which only pro-Union "representatives" would be authorized to speak, vote or have any part in the assembly.

---

[23] Rogers, H. John "Political Corruption." e-WV: The West Virginia Encyclopedia. 18 June 2013. Web. 15 February 2015.

[24] "West Virginia Corruption Risk Report Card" State Integrity Investigation. Web. 20 September 2015.

How could the assembly claim to be fulfilling the will of the people of Virginia or even Western Virginians, when the state's voters chose secession by more than a 60,000 vote margin?

How could they represent the counties in West Virginia which voted to secede from the Union – yet refuse to allow any person who shared these beliefs to have any part in the assembly?

Recognizing the Wheeling Convention's failure to adequately represent the people of Western Virginia, Cabell County's representative, J. Madison Laidley, refused to take the loyalty oath and left Wheeling, rejecting the convention and its claims to serve as Virginia's sitting government.

### *State Officials Selected*

By another ordinance the convention moved forward with a bill that stated, "A Governor, Lieutenant-Governor and Attorney General for the State of Virginia, shall be elected by this convention…"

On June 20, 1861, the convention elected the officers provided for in the ordinance. Of these officers, Fairmont attorney Francis H. Pierpont was selected to serve as governor, Daniel Polsley as lieutenant governor and James S. Wheat as attorney general.

All three of these men were ambitious lawyers who snatched the opportunity to achieve statewide offices – offices that had hitherto been off limits to them due to voting demographics which weighted toward candidates from other regions of the state.

John S. Carlile, the driving force behind the first Wheeling Convention and Waitman T. Willey were selected to represent the Restored Government of Virginia in the United States Senate.

Harrison County's John Carlile had already established a name for himself among loyalists and could be trusted to represent the convention's true interest, the creation of a new state, or so they thought.

Like Pierpont, Willey was a graduate of Madison College (later Allegheny College) at Uniontown, Pennsylvania, and though deeply involved in and passionate about politics, he had a long history of being rejected by the sovereign voters of Western Virginia:

- In 1840 Willey was defeated in his run for the Virginia General Assembly.

- In 1852 Willey was defeated in his run for the U.S. Congress
- In 1859 Willey was defeated in his run for Lt. Governor of Virginia

The Wheeling Convention circumvented the will of the voters in nearly all of West Virginia's communities, propelled those who were previously deemed unelectable to high offices, in Willey's case, the United States Senate.

### *A Courtship with the Federal Government*

In 1842, following an incident in Rhode Island where two separate assemblies were claiming to be the sovereign government of the state, the Supreme Court ruled that the Federal government had the right to decide which of the two competing governments of a state was the legitimate and sovereign power.

Recognizing this relatively recent court ruling, the lawyers who had gathered in Wheeling set out to portray themselves as being the sovereign Government of Virginia and had planned to take their case to the United States Supreme Court if necessary.

With a Federal government angry at the Richmond legislature for snubbing them, choosing instead to ally with the "Cotton Republic," attorneys in the Northwestern Panhandle believed obtaining recognition from Washington as being the true Virginia government would be a fairly easy task – after all, the Union government was in a state of war against the authorities in Richmond and recognizing the assembly in Wheeling would hurl a severe blow against that assembly.

The Civil War raised a multitude of constitutional issues. The general attitude of the Lincoln Administration with each of these dilemmas was that the survival of the country was at stake, therefore circumstances often justified disobeying the constitution in order to preserve it.

Even when it came to West Virginia's statehood, an act we will speak about in greater detail in the coming chapters, Lincoln stated:

"The division of a state is dreaded as a precedent, but a measure expedient by a war is no precedent for times of peace."

Though fully aware that the assembly gathered in Wheeling was largely comprised of political speculators who failed to represent the true will of the people, the Lincoln Administration reluctantly offered limited recognition to the Restored Government of Virginia – following the old adage, "An enemy of my enemy is a friend."

In the days ahead, the Federal government made an exception for the postal service to continue its operation in northwestern Virginia (the Washington government had ceased the postal service's operation throughout all other seceded states). This act alone was all the recognition the Wheeling Convention needed to declare itself the lawfully "Restored Government of Virginia," claiming its sovereignty over all 147 counties of Virginia.

## West Virginia: Funded by a Bank Robbery

By late-June, the Wheeling Convention had found itself in a unique legal conundrum:

On one hand, the convention was declaring itself to be the legal and sovereign government of Virginia.

On the other hand, the convention had received only limited recognition from the Executive Branch of the Federal Government: the Secretary of War had corresponded with the convention's "Governor," but the Secretary stopped short of fully recognizing them as being the sovereign authority of Virginia.

Though the Lincoln Administration appreciated their loyalty to the Union, the constitutional crisis the very existence of the Wheeling assembly presented was a battle the administration was not prepared to engage in nor desired.

The vast majority of the "representatives" had not been elected and more than four out of five Virginia counties were not provided any type of representation in the body, therefore, any claims to be the true government of Virginia could not be legally substantiated.

Lacking any true legal authority, including the power of taxation, the convention, which was by this time claiming to serve as the Government of the Commonwealth of Virginia, was in desperate need of funding, after all, the assembly recently voted to pay themselves for their "service" to the people of Virginia… despite having no treasury from which to move forward with this act.

To create a state treasury, Governor Pierpont and delegate Peter Van Winkle secured $10,000 in a loan from Wheeling banks on their personal endorsement.

Despite this loan, the newly created government would require a lot more capital than that to ensure its survival.

Officials in Wheeling began to actively liquidate tangible property which belonged to the Virginia government in Richmond – claiming authority over the property due to being the "Restored Government of Virginia."

Despite their claims of sovereignty over the entire state, Western Virginia was a lawless land in the summer of 1861 and the sitting authority in each town was often the army with the most infantrymen nearby.

With the Restored Government continuing to suffer from insufficient funds, Presley Hale, a representative from the community of Weston, in Lewis County, approached the appointed governor and informed him of a massive stockpile of gold that was presently being housed in a bank in his hometown.

The gold belonged to the Commonwealth of Virginia and had been placed in the bank by the Richmond government to pay local workers who were building the Trans-Allegheny Asylum, later known as the Weston State Hospital.

Hale argued that this money belonged to Virginia and since the Wheeling Convention was now the Restored Government of Virginia, the gold was theirs.

The total amount of the stockpile was $27,000, equal to roughly a quarter-million dollars in 2015 money.

PHOTO: The completed Trans-Allegheny Lunatic Asylum, subsequently known as the Weston State Hospital, a psychiatric facility operated from 1864 until 1994 by the State of West Virginia. *(Courtesy Tim Kiser)*

Under Governor Pierpont's order, the Seventh Ohio Infantry drove deep into the state and marched into the town of Weston early in the morning of June 30, 1861.

After having marched 25 miles from Clarksburg the night before, members of the Ohio infantry entered the town at the break of dawn and immediately began rousing the townspeople from their beds with a deafening rendition of "The Star-Spangled Banner."

As residents, nearly all of whom were still in their bedclothes, ran into the streets in a panic, the invading army marched straight to the bank where the gold was being stored and demanded all of it.

Robert McCandlish, the bank's teller, was driven from his bed and ordered to turn over the gold immediately.

McCandlish asked if some money could be kept to pay the workers, as it was intended, but his request was denied by the invading Ohio army.

Realizing any resistance would be futile, the defeated teller then reached into the vault and handed over twenty-seven leather pouches to Union Army officials, each of which contained $1,000 in gold.

From Weston, the gold was loaded onto a heavily guarded wagon and carried to Clarksburg, where it was transferred to a train which transported the loot up to Wheeling.

Though the gold proved valuable in the establishment of the Restored Government's treasury, the manner in which it was taken from the people of Weston remained a source of contention for decades to come.

One of the first official acts of what would become the State of West Virginia was to rob its own citizens of their wages in order to compensate politicians – an unfortunate trend that has often been repeated in the state government's history.

Regrettably, stealing from its own citizens the fruits of their labors was not the worst atrocity committed that summer morning by Ohio soldiers, under the command of Western Virginia's self-appointed governor.

In addition to robbing the working West Virginians who had been laboring in the construction of the facility, the foreign invaders, under the Restored Government's command swept through the town and seized any individuals suspected of holding Confederate sympathies.

Fathers, sons, community leaders and sole income earners were separated from their families and deprived of their most basic constitutional right – the right to free thought.. the same rights the invading army arresting the free citizens of Lewis County were supposedly fighting to protect.

The events of this early summer morning in 1861 set a dangerous precedence in American history and eventually led to even more unimaginable atrocities throughout the nation: By rounding up and arresting those whose political ideologies differed from the President's, the soldiers of Ohio's 7th Infantry plunged the nation unto a course where one's own personal sympathies (even if they were never acted upon) could be reason enough to have him arrested by Federal authorities.

The country that was founded by freethinking men such as Thomas Jefferson and Benjamin Franklin, had entered into an era where one dare not share his true opinions for fear of being arrested by the ruling establishment.

Sadly, this terrible path would eventually lead to the arrest of media members in the months to come by officials in the Lincoln Administration, as well as the incarceration of Japanese-Americans less than a century later – simply due to their ancestry. These heinous actions all had their origins in a command issued by Governor Francis Pierpont of the Restored Government of Virginia – the forerunner of the State of West Virginia.

In the decades ahead, as the Wheeling Convention's "Restored Government of Virginia" evolved into the State of West Virginia, the state government's officials would continue down this inhumane path, siding with big money over the interests of their own working-class citizens time and time again.

This appalling misalignment of priorities would serve as the root causes for horrific events of bloodshed in the generations to come.

Events such as the Battle of Blair Mountain, the Matewan Massacre and the bloodshed at Paint Creek can all be traced to government officials in the State of West Virginia, originally the Restored Government of Virginia, placing their own personal interests above the will of their citizens.

The most heartbreaking reality is that the ghastly tragedies that have defined West Virginia's history for over a century could have been easily avoided, if only the people of the mountains had an honest government, sadly, the plant that was to become the state's government was corrupt to its root – owing its founding to the lies laid forth by power hungry politicians of the Wheeling Convention.

Though the state's motto may boldly proclaim that "Mountaineers are Always Free," in reality, thanks in large part to the unlawful precedence set by the 1861 assembly, West Virginia's mountaineers have historically been the most oppressed people in the nation.

Chapter
Seven

# The "Restored Government"
# West Virginia's Corrupt Root

The men who assembled in Wheeling, Virginia, in June of 1861 did so not in order to restore the government of Virginia back to its original place in the Union, for had that been their goal, we may very well be proclaiming their goodness today.

Unfortunately, this was not the case, instead, their desire was to destroy the government of Virginia; all the while feigning to Federal authorities a false desire to save the Old Dominion from its prodigal ways.

Their final goal, however, was not the preservation of Virginia, but instead its obliteration.

In May of 1861, Harrison County's John Carlile made no qualms in sharing his final desire with convention members in the First Wheeling Convention: the creation of a new state.

97

His desires to form a new state were met with stiff opposition – even from many committed abolitionists and staunch Unionists.

Realizing the unpopularity of their end-goal, organizers of the Second Wheeling Convention set out to redefine the argument in the weeks leading up to their meeting. All but ceasing their calls for a new state, they instead focused upon the "restoration of Virginia."

Despite what many of the coordinators of the assembly were saying to the media, or what the state government has rigidly been teaching for the past 150 years, the average resident living in Western Virginia had lost his desire to form a new state once the Virginia Constitution of 1851 went into law; the document had squelched most of the issues westerners had been raising and presented a fair and proportionate government for all people of the Commonwealth.

By the spring of 1861, there may have been pockets of the Commonwealth opposed to slavery, but the advocates for dividing the state in two were Virginia's northwestern politicians. It was their desire to see the grand old state dissected and for no other reason than to increase the likelihood of them being elected to a statewide office.

Winning a state of fifty counties – when your region serves as the principal city – was a far easier order than winning a state of 147 counties whose capital and main population centers lie hundreds of miles away.


## The Constitutional Hurdle

As is often the case for those in government with some nefarious scheme aimed at personal gain – against the majority's will – the United States Constitution presented the greatest obstacle for Carlile and his hoard of "new state men" gathered in Wheeling.

Article IV of the founding document expressly forbade the creation of a new state within the borders of another state without the approval of the original state.

The founders of West Virginia knew that any hope for creating the State of Kanawha, Western Virginia, New Virginia, West Virginia (or whatever the many individual factions were desiring to call the new government) would only be possible if the Commonwealth of Virginia authorized this division of their own state – and with the Old Dominion now engaged in a bitter war with the government of the United States, the likelihood of the legislators in Richmond voting to allow a handful of pro-Union counties to leave was virtually non-existent.

Even Edward Bates, the United States Attorney General who was privy of the June Convention's true desire, authored this dire caution to the assembly:

*"The formation of a new State out of Western Virginia is an original act of revolution….Any attempt to carry it out involves a plain breech of both the Constitutions of Virginia and of the Nation."*[25]

According to Bates, the supreme attorney in the entire nation and Lincoln appointee, creating a new state in Western Virginia would be an illegal act, breaking both the Constitution of Virginia, as well as the Constitution of the United States of America.

Undeterred, by the fact that their actions were seen throughout the nation as being unconstitutional, the men of the Second Wheeling Convention devised an audacious and farfetched plan:

They would first seek to establish a newly reorganized government of Virginia. This government would be made up entirely of northwestern Union sympathizers whose true desire was the creation of a separate state in the northwestern portion of Virginia.

Once the reorganized government had been recognized by Federal authorities, the legislators of the interim regime would then vote to authorize the state's western counties to secede from the Commonwealth, effectively circumventing the Constitutional requirement that a state could only be subdivided when the sovereign government of that state authorized it to do so.

No one truly believed the Wheeling Convention held the legal right to act as the provisional government of Virginia, much less authorize the creation of a brand new state; however, in the summer of 1861, the nation had far greater battles to worry about than political trickeries taking place on the banks of the Ohio River.

---

[25] *The New York Times.* "Western Virginia.; Opinion of Attorney General Bates on the Proposition to Divide the State." Published: August 20, 1861.

Jeremy T.K. Farley

# The Restored Government of Virginia

What began as the Second Wheeling Convention had transformed itself, almost overnight, into the "Restored Government of Virginia," going so far as to proclaim its capital to be in the embattled city of Richmond, though the members agreed that circumstances beyond their control hindered them from actually meeting in Richmond and that Wheeling should serve as the temporary capital city for the exiled government.

All of this was done in the face of fierce objection from countless people living in what would become West Virginia, as well as many serving in the United States government.

Several of the staunchest of Lincolnites opposed the dissection of Virginia, viewing it as being both unlawful and unnecessary.

*The New York Commercial Advertiser* was incredibly concerned over the prospect of having Virginia bisected:

"Constitutionally the western counties had no right to secede and the people should not furnish Charleston [South Carolina] and Richmond with an argument which might be employed with fatal effect against the Federal Government.

"Only two-sevenths of the delegates were in favor of dividing the state," declared the *Advertiser*.

## A People Not Convinced

It was not uncommon throughout the American Civil War for one son to leave the family home place and head north to join the Union army while his brother went south to ally himself with the Confederacy.

Stories abound of Yankee fathers searching bloody battlefields for the corpses of their sons who were clad in southern-grey and West Virginia is no exception – even the very founders of the Restored Government were not immune to this discrepancy of loyalties.

Among the men of West Virginia who experienced divided loyalties was Senator Waitman T. Willey.

A staunch loyalist, Willey served as the Restored Government's first of two senators. His half-brother William Goshorn, however, was a fierce secessionist who fought for the Confederacy.

Throughout the American Civil War, West Virginia served as a contested borderland filled with unionists and secessionists, who battled for every square foot of the Mountains.

For any person to say that the region overwhelmingly sided with the Union or with the Southern Confederacy would be a gross inaccuracy on either part. Western Virginia was, as it is today, a watershed.

True to the ancient quote, "History is written by the victors," in the years to follow the War Between the States, Union officials and West Virginia apologists set out to re-write the Civil War narrative concerning the Mountain State, alleging the ratio of Union enlisted soldiers to their Confederate counterparts from West Virginia as having been five to one.

For years, this commonly accepted and unquestioned statistic served as the "gotcha" evidence needed by those who sought to defend the manner by which the state was created, using the tried and true defense, "the end justifies the means."

A century and a half later, historians have now uncovered hard truths which reveal the five to one ratio was nothing more than a bold and outright lie.

In his February 2015 article, "Confederate Soldiers in West Virginia," Jack L. Dickinson wrote:

"It is difficult to determine the number of Confederate soldiers from West Virginia. Records were destroyed when the Confederate capitol at Richmond burned, and regimental rosters were captured or destroyed in battle. For decades the most often quoted number of West Virginia Confederates was 7,000. More recent research, using sources such as the Compiled Service Records, shows that 16,000 to 18,000 men from West Virginia fought for the Confederacy... [the] loyalties of the West Virginia counties were not as unbalanced in favor of the Union as was once thought."[26]


# Lies, Deception and Political Trickery

In addition to giving itself the authority to name a governor, lieutenant governor and attorney general – all of whom, like most of

---

[26] Dickinson, Jack L. "Confederate Soldiers in West Virginia." e-WV: The West Virginia Encyclopedia. 13 June 2011. Web. 20 September 2015.

the convention members themselves, were never elected by the will of the people – the convention also instituted a provision which gave itself the authority to "re-establish" the Virginia Senate and Virginia House of Delegates; even though these two bodies were undeniably intact and functioning in Richmond.

Though the convention attempted to act like their assembly was the true legislative branch of government for the Commonwealth, the reality is that even they recognized the council had no true authority.

Evidence of their lack in confidence is clearly seen in the following clause of the Ordinance for the Reorganization of the State Government:

*"A majority of the members of each branch thus qualified . . . shall be competent to pass any act specified in the twenty-seventh section of the fourth article of the constitution. (This section of the Virginia Constitution provides for the creation or discharge of any state debt.)."*[27]

It is difficult to understand why any such authorization was necessary if, as the convention assumed, the General Assembly created in Wheeling was the only legal legislative body of Virginia. Why specify what powers it could exercise when such powers were clearly enumerated in the constitution of the state?

How could the constitution of Virginia be acknowledged as the law of the Commonwealth under one set of conditions and repudiated in another... in the same document, *The Ordinance for the Reorganization of the State Government?*

The fact that the convention even thought it necessary to specifically authorize the newly created "state legislature" to create a state debt is a virtual admission of the weakness of its position – it is a commonly understood fact that legislative bodies possess the power to oversee the government's finances.

---

[27] *An Ordinance for the Reorganization of the State Government.* June 14, 1861.

## Disregarding the Will of the People

The assembled convention passed an ordinance stating that all county and state officers were to take the oath of allegiance to the United States Government.

If any refused to do this, the governor should provide for a special election to fill the vacancy. Where no officers could be found to conduct the election, the governor was given the power to make permanent appointments.

With Confederate forces controlling nearly four-fifths of the entire state of Virginia, the Wheeling Convention had seeded to F.H. Pierpont, who was acting as the head of the Commonwealth's "Restored Government," an unmatched level of power – a power in which they themselves never truly had the right to seed in the first place.

By their measure, Pierpont had been "authorized" to hand pick roughly 80% of the members of the state's legislative body – allowing he and his cohorts an unspeakable opportunity to annex virtually full control over Union-held Virginia.

The very moment the article was passed that gave Pierpont total control to handpick representative for a county hundreds of miles away, counties in which he had never even stepped foot, all hope of an honest and representative form of government for West Virginia was dashed away.

The premise of this book isn't that the Union was wrong or that Old Virginia was right, but that the creation of West Virginia was illegal and done for the purpose of pleasing the political desires of a handful of politicians from Northern West Virginia.

Rather than act in the interests of the citizens of the mountains, the men of the body calling themselves the "Restored Government of Virginia" were actually doing everything but represent the people's interests: They stole $27,000 from West Virginia workers, arrested free-citizens based upon their personal sympathies and refused to acknowledge the will of the people throughout most – or at least half – of Western Virginia.

## An Appeal to the People

The convention adjourned on June 25, 1861, scheduling to return on August 6th.

A long address had been drawn up and was now sent throughout the state, declaring:

*The delegates now assembled in convention at Wheeling deem it proper to address their fellow citizens throughout the commonwealth in explanation and vindication of the course they have unanimously felt it incumbent upon them to pursue...*

*In this state of things the day arrived when the people were to vote for or against the secession ordinance. Threats of personal injury ... or other intimidations were used in every county in the state. Judges charged the Grand Juries that opposition to this Union would be punished as treason and the armed partisans of the conspirators arrested, plundered, and exiled peaceable citizens for no other crime than their adherence to the Union.*[28]

Defending the June Wheeling Convention's authority, the address conceded that the May Wheeling Convention had no authority and was nothing more than an assembly of concerned citizens; however, the proclamation stated that the June Wheeling Convention had the authority to reorganize the Virginia government.

This is an interesting legal argument, as the June Wheeling Convention was called to assemble by the May Wheeling Convention.

If the May Wheeling Convention lacked any true authority, then how could the June Wheeling Convention, which was convened by the May Convention, hold any more power, let alone assume the authority of the entire government of the Commonwealth of Virginia?

It would seem that since the second convention had been called together by the first, they would be equally irregular and sterile.

The address went on to state:

---

[28] *Address Objecting to Secession, to the People of Virginia by the Delegates Assembled in Convention at Wheeling.* June 24, 1861.

*The number of counties represented is thirty-four and we have assurance that several which are now with us in spirit will ere long be present by their regularly appointed delegates... Several of the delegates present escaped from their counties at the risk of their lives while others are still detained at home by force or menace.*

This concession alone is enough to prove that many of the counties which were drug into the illegal state of West Virginia did not have any desire to leave the Commonwealth of Virginia nor join a Union state.

According to the convention's address to the people, many of the "delegates" meeting in Wheeling to create a new state were doing so against the will of the citizens they supposedly represented.

When representatives have "escaped from their counties at the risk of their lives" in order to attend a convention the townspeople did not wish for them to attend, it is more than safe to say that the people's will was not adequately represented.

**A False Calm**

Though the Second Wheeling Convention's address to the people of Virginia clearly stated that it was the goal of many to form a new state – this was a truth the officials who gathered in the northern West Virginia community could not hide (they had shown their true cards in the May convention) – they also attempted to downplay the possibility of such a drastic event actually becoming reality.

Though the June convention had cleared the groundwork for the erection of a new state, many people were intentionally deceived into believing that all thoughts of breaking away from the east had been forsaken and the group gathering in Wheeling were merely interested in preserving the Commonwealth of Virginia's government – in the eyes of the Federals – for the duration of the war.

On June 10, 1861, *The Pittsburgh Chronicle* stated that it had received "reliable information" to the effect that the idea of dividing Virginia into two separate pieces had been abandoned.

We do not know the sources the Western Pennsylvania reporter was relying upon or deemed as "reliable," however, we do know that the information was anything but "reliable."

In fact, the ruling clique in Wheeling had laid out a definite plan of campaign for creating a new state.

Far from having a change of heart, the politicians who were outwardly demanding for a new state during the First Wheeling Convention were now only whispering of their ultimate plan.

Following the Second Convention, leaders sought to tone down their public rhetoric, fearing that to only pursue such a proposal would only serve only to arouse the opponents of the new state in Congress and in Western Virginia herself – instead, the State of West Virginia would be created under the cover of darkness, behind closed doors, and illegally. Setting a precedent in the state's politics that has yet to be overcome.

The oligarchical nature of the new provisional government made it possible for its leaders to carry on their work with the utmost secrecy, and the absolute indifference of the northwestern counties to what the Pierpont government was doing made it easy for the self-appointed officials to remain in undisputed possession of the Northern government – setting the ball in motion for America's coup d'état, the disruption of Virginia.

## A Secret Legislature

On July 2, 1861, there assembled in Wheeling a nondescript body calling itself the legislature of Virginia. No record of its proceedings has ever come to light and only the vaguest information is obtainable regarding its actions.

According to the laws of Virginia, elections for Senators and delegates to the General Assembly were to occur on the fourth Thursday of May every second year.

The ordinance passed by the Richmond Convention on April 17, 1861, while forbidding the election of representatives to Congress, said nothing regarding the election of members to the state legislature – that body remained intact.

Thus on the May 23, 1861, while the people were ratifying the ordinance of secession, they also elected a new General Assembly.

Then came the establishment of the Wheeling government and the call by "Governor" Pierpont for the assembling of the legislature.

Richmond was the place designated by the constitution for the holding of legislative sessions and while the Governor was empowered to call extra-sessions, he could not change the capital from one city to another. Despite these technical legalities, the "new state" officials leapt over this constitutional barrier just as they had brushed aside so many others.

To act first and discuss later was their very effective mode of procedure, and to their strict adherence to this plan can the formation of the State of West Virginia be attributed.

The Wheeling newspapers are strangely silent as to the doings of the rump legislature. They do not give even the names of the senators and delegates who were present or what districts were represented.

At the opening session three senators were present: Joseph Gist, representing the Panhandle district; James Carskardon from the district composed of Hampshire, Hardy and Morgan counties; and C. J. Stuart, representing Ritchie, Doddridge, Harrison, Pleasants, and Wood counties.

Twelve members of the House of Delegates answered the roll call the opening day.

On July 26, 1861, the *Wheeling Intelligencer* stated, editorially:

*We would be glad if they would settle the question among themselves down there as to whether or not they really are the Legislature of Virginia. This little question has been up in nearly all the discussions of the House and we hope some conclusion may be reached before adjournment.*

Judging from the number of voters from the assembly who participated in the election of United States Senators, it seems probable that the largest number of senators and delegates in the first session of the loyal legislature never exceeded thirty-eight – the constitutional number was 206.

# An Unrecognized Government

The only authority the Wheeling Convention had to declare themselves the "Restored Government of Virginia" was their very own words – nothing more.

As the month of June drug on, support for the convention and its power clamoring, unelected "legislators" diminished greatly.

*The Morgantown Star* became a strong opponent of the provisional government and declared that the members of the convention had been bought off by New York brokers.[29]

West Virginia had always been cursed with conventions, whether held in Richmond or Wheeling and most in the state viewed the convention gathered in Wheeling during the summer of 1861 to be just another meeting of politicians full of hot air.

So opposed were residents of central and southern West Virginia to the Wheeling Convention that a circular letter from Lewis County was sent throughout the state during mid-June, urging a counter-convention to be held at Lewisburg for the purpose of checkmating the Wheeling government.

*The Wheeling Intelligencer* reported on July 30th that the counties were taking up the work of reorganization very slowly. It comments sorrowfully on the defeat of the North at Bull Run being wildly celebrated throughout the central and southern parts of West Virginia.

## The Story of Judge Thompson

Tucked safely away in the Northwestern Panhandle of Western Virginia, the Wheeling Convention declared every office in the entire state to have been vacated and tasked themselves with filling these "vacant" positions.

Among these "vacated" offices was that of Judge George W. Thompson, a graduate of the University of Virginia.

Thompson was a former Congressman who had been elected to serve as judge of the 20th district of Virginia in 1852.

A staunch unionist, Thompson served as one of the earliest vocal Lincoln supporters in all of Virginia.

On October 31, 1861, Thompson wrote the Illinois senator, urging him to "secure able and upright men to aid you in executing your well settled & calm resolve to save the Union by a concession which shall not be unworthy of so momentous occasion."

When the Virginia secession ordinance was passed on April 17, 1861, Judge Thompson denounced it.

If any man shared the spoken vision of the Wheeling Convention, the supposed preservation of Virginia under the Union, it was Judge Thompson.

---

[29] McGregor. p. 219

Thompson's loyalties to Lincoln and the Union, however, would fail to be enough to garner him the support of the Restored Government of Virginia or its tyrant-governor Francis H. Pierpont.

Attempting to consolidate as much power as possible, the Pierpont Administration set out to identify and destroy supposed political adversaries, even if those individuals stood on the side of the Union or Lincoln. For the founders of the Restored Government, loyalty to the Union was not an issue – they desired men who would sit quietly as Pierpont and his henchmen consolidated total power in Wheeling.

Judge Thompson was outspoken, trusted by the people and above all else, opposed to the division of Virginia, all three of these attributes placed him on a collision course with Pierpont.

Under Pierpont's command, the Union army roaming through Western Virginia – comprised mainly of Ohio and Pennsylvania soldiers – removed the elected judge and had him replaced with an unelected magistrate of the unelected governor's choosing.

Livid by the fact that he had been removed from his office by an unelected body,

Judge George W. Thompson

headed by an unelected man who claimed to be the governor of Virginia, Judge Thompson issued a letter to the United States Senate and the Supreme Court, arguing that the "Restored Government" was fueled by nothing more than "the ambition of a few men in political combination..."[30]

Judge Thompson had made Pierpont's shortlist of political adversaries following a speech made on May 10, 1861, in which the judge declared, "Whoever attempts and makes any overt acts toward establishing without authority of the state legislature any government

---

[30] *Documents of Virginia 1861-62, Part 5, No 52.*

within the limits of the state separate from the existing government, or shall hold or execute any office in such usurped government, or shall profess allegiance of fidelity to it, or shall resist the execution of the laws...is guilty of treason."[31]

For Judge Thompson, a man of the utmost character, his eventual undoing would come due to his insistence in following the letter of the law.

Just weeks after making his address on May 10th, which was met with the sharpest of criticisms from those in Wheeling, the judge managed to draw equal hatred from Confederate sympathizers when he ordered Confederate militiamen in Western Virginia to disperse.

The judge's resolve to interpret the law without any prejudices to the "Wheeling cause" or the "Richmond cause" left him with few personal friends and numerous political enemies – from both sides of the fight.

The following month, officials from the newly established "Restored Government" approached Thompson and demand that he take a loyalty oath.

Though the Western Virginia judge had no objection to swearing allegiance to the United States government, he vehemently objected to pledging to "uphold and defend the Government of Virginia as vindicated and restored by the Convention which assembled in Wheeling on the 11th day of June, 1861."[32]

Judge Thompson considered the Wheeling government to be against the will of the people and illegal, therefore he refused to take the oath.

Having his salary withheld by the Richmond government due to his order for Confederate troops to disband and having orders from the Wheeling government to be forcefully removed from office if necessary, Thompson found himself the enemy of both governments (claiming to be Virginia's) in the summer of 1861.

Despite his early loyalties falling solely to the side of Lincoln, both of the judge's two sons sided with the Confederacy, viewing Virginia as their native land and committing themselves to its defense.

---

[31] *Wheeling Intelligencer*, May 11, 1861.

[32] *New York Times*. "VIRGINIA.; The Restored Government of Virginia-- History of the New State of Things." June 26, 1864.

Thompson's loyalties, too, would soon be shaken following a round of legal battles against Pierpont and his despotic regime. The judge was eventually arrested by Pierpont's thought police and carried away to Camp Chase.

With her husband arrested by the Union Army and her sons gone to war in defense of the Confederacy, Thompson's wife fled to safety in Richmond: escaping what was becoming an ever increasingly oppressive military regime in Western Virginia. A regime headed by an unchecked, tyrannical and self-appointed governor.

On January 13, 1862, the *Richmond Daily Dispatch* provided an account of Thompson's escape:

Among the refugees recently arrived here from Northwestern Virginia, are Mrs. Judge Thompson, of Wheeling, and Dr. N. W. White, of Wellsburg, in Brooke county.

Judge Thompson was at a very late period of the rupture with the North a strong Union man, and wrote a pamphlet against Secession. It was inferred that he would join the Union party, both by the advocates of the Ordinance of Secession and the Lincolnites. But the Northern Government went too far for the Judge. He revolted at their outrages upon Constitutional law and liberty and refused to submit to their authority. He refused to take the oath of allegiance to the Federal Government and was immediately deposed by Pierpont, the bogus Governor of Western Virginia, and an election ordered to fill the office of Circuit Judge, in this manner vacated.

A fifth rate county court lawyer was elected, and all unfit as he is, has entered upon the discharge of the duties of the high office.

Mrs. Thompson is a devoted Southern lady, and successfully escaping from the land of tyranny, recently arrived in safety here, where she has been much afflicted by the death of a gallant son who fell in the late battle at Allegheny mountain. She has yet another son in the service of the South.

West Virginia writer Bobby Lee Arrington, author of *West Virginia - The Other History*, has invested an incredible amount of time

111

in highlighting the state's "other history" and has offered a collection of newspaper accounts of Judge Thompson's saga to the public:

**Aug. 8, 1862 –** *Richmond Daily Dispatch:*
S. S. Mann, a very intelligent Yankee, the sutler of the 16th Massachusetts, captured in the brilliant cavalry dash made by Gen. Stuart, has been paroled for sixty days to go the North and negotiate an exchange of himself for Judge Geo. W. Thompson, a citizen of Wheeling, recently seized by the Yankees for disloyalty, and a Yankee sutler named Everlith, now here, for Samuel Price, Esq, a leading lawyer of Greenbrier, member of the late Convention, seized by the Yankees during one of their recent raids in that vicinity." Samuel Price had been a delegate to the Richmond convention the previous year, and later would be a U.S. senator from West Virginia.

**Oct. 16, 1862 –** *Richmond Daily Dispatch:*
By the arrival yesterday of two ladies from Wheeling, we have obtained some information of the condition of affairs in Pierpont's dominions.
That demagogue, who by accident presides over the people of Northwestern Virginia, is exercising a tyranny more odious and oppressive, if possible, than that of his master, Lincoln.
A short time since, Judge George W. Thompson, of the Wheeling Judicial Circuit, was released from a long and tedious imprisonment at Camp Chase, and returned to his home in Wheeling. The day after his arrival, Pierpont had him re-arrested, and at last accounts he was still in prison.
Hon. Lewis Steenrod, another prominent citizen of Ohio county, was arrested by order of Pierpont on the same day.
Mr. S. has been in exceedingly delicate health for some time, and his recovery is not regarded, yet Pierpont was unfeeling enough to send him word that he intended to make him take the oath of allegiance before he died.

Other acts of oppression are related, which have caused the loyal people of that section to long more earnestly than ever for the day of deliverance.

Bobby Lee Arrington writes, "In late April 1863 Gov. Pierpoint ordered another arrest of Judge Thompson for the purpose of prisoner exchange. There were no charges against him and his arrest was for his use as a hostage."[33]

Arrington went on to state, "On June 25th Judge Thompson was granted bail in the amount of $5,000 upon condition that he return home and remain there. On the 29th the hearing continued, with the defense demanding evidence of any disloyal act committed by Judge Thompson."

According to the *Wheeling Intelligencer*:

Mr. Caldwell replied that Thompson had refused to take the oath of allegiance. It was the mixed oath which he had refused to take. Mr. Caldwell insisted that he had refused to take the oath and that Col. Darr had so testified.

Judge Thompson then advanced towards Mr. Caldwell with apparently hostile intentions, when Mr. Caldwell looked at him and said, 'You dare to lay a hand on me.' The court directed the Marshal to take charge of the gentleman when Deputy Irwin came forward and the little passage was cut short.

The following page contains a letter to the United States Secretary of War from J. Holt, Judge – Advocate General.

The letter speaks of the plight of Judge Thompson and lays out the case against Francis Pierpont who, by mid-1863, was West Virginia's unchallenged dictator:

---

[33] Arrington, Bobby Lee. "Pierpont's Bastille – The Trials of Judge Thompson." Web. 20 September 2015.

*July 31, 1863*

*The Secretary Of War:*

The prisoner, George W. Thompson, appears to have been arrested by the provost-marshal of Western Virginia, or by soldiers acting under his direction. It does not, however, appear on what grounds or for what purpose the arrest was made, though from the returns of the jailer it would seem that he claimed to hold him as a hostage by order of the Governor as constitutional commander-in-chief of militia.

The provost-marshal should be required to report at once for what offense and by what authority the prisoner was arrested, and the report when received will probably enable the Secretary to dispose of the case. This course is the more obviously proper since there is reason to apprehend that this arrest was made in violation of the declared purpose of the Department in reference to the prisoner. Major Turner, in speaking for the Secretary, stated to the provost-marshal that in case the prisoner had done nothing disloyal since his return he was not to be molested for anything that had occurred prior to his exchange, and Judge Jackson alleges in his opinion that the prisoner has not been charged as guilty of any disloyal practices since the time named.

The seizing and holding of hostages in reprisal for captures made by the enemy is certainly an exercise of the war-making power, belonging exclusively to the General Government, and which cannot be shared by the Governor of the States without leading to deplorable complications.

J. HOLT, *Judge-Advocate- General*

Despite being enemy of the state to both the Virginia government in Richmond, as well as to the "Virginia government" in Wheeling, Judge Thompson continued to exercise some political power – even from prison.

In the summer of 1863, the former Virginia judge successfully arranged to have Gov. Francis Pierpont arrested as he traveled into Ohio.

The August 10, 1863, edition of the *New York Daily Tribune* covers this story:

A Wheeling paper says that Gov. Pierpont of West Virginia was arrested in Bridgport by the Sheriff of Belmont County, and held to bail in the sum of $10,000 for his appearance in the next term of court held for that County. The charge preferred against him is the false imprisonment in Wheeling of Judge Geo. Thompson.

In the end, the Belmont County Court let Pierpont go free, but the judge did manage to cause a great deal of embarrassment to the acting governor, as well as the Wheeling government.

Judge Thompson would not be freed from prison until July 16, 1864, three months following the surrender of Lee at Appomattox, Judge Thompson. His crime – refusing to take a loyalty oath to the Wheeling government.

By the time Judge Thompson was released, the leaders in West Virginia's panhandle accomplished their ultimate goal, the realization of the State of West Virginia.

Two years later, Thompson filed a lawsuit against Pierpont for false imprisonment.

Though Pierpont was no longer its governor, the State of West Virginia appropriated funds for Pierpont to defend himself and the judge lost his suit in a pro-West Virginia, Lincoln appointed court.

Bobby Lee Arrington's *West Virginia - The Other History*, closes its account of the Judge Thompson saga by offering a snippet of an 1875 interview between a reporter of the *Wheeling Register* and the near 70-year-old ex-Virginia judge, George W. Thompson:

Judge Thompson: "I have seen twenty great States arise and become parts of the republic, where there was wilderness when I was a boy. I have seen an empire established where there was a republic, after I had passed the prime of manhood."

Interviewer:      "That is strong language. You do not mean to say that we have the empire?"

Judge Thompson: "I mean to say, that when the first irreversible step is taken of deliberately surrendering the liberties of the people to the armed authority of a President, at his own discretion; to suspend the habeas corpus, and to intrude his soldiery into the States, and control or interfere with their domestic management of their own affairs, the republican principle is surrendered and the empire is inaugurated. The forms of the republic will remain long after the substance of republicanism is eaten out of their vitalities. It was Greece; it was Rome; it is the turning point of American life."

Chapter
Eight

# Carving Up The Map

July 4, 1861, marked the nation's eighty-fifth birthday, however, the mood in Washington, D.C., was far from celebratory in nature.

The concentrated forces of Confederate General P.G.T. Beauregard and his Union counterpart, General Winfield Scott, had yet to meet on the battlefield and the entire city was in the highest state of alert as residents lived with a constant fear of a Confederate invasion at any moment.

Mary Henry, daughter of the Smithsonian Institution's first secretary, recorded a diary of the day's events:

*It is Independence Day, hallowed & dear to the hearts of the American people but the Birth Festival of our republic awakens sad thoughts as well as patriotic feelings.*

*There was a grand parade of the NY regiments early in the morning that state has already sent 50,000 men to the aid of the Government & is ready to provide more if they are needed.*

*At twelve o'clock, Congress opened we went up some time before in order to procure seats, but found very few people in the Senate galleries, the House was crowded...*

*The situation of the few Democrats here now is very disagreeable. It was very sad as the Senators took their seats -- to miss the old familiar faces, the tones that had only a few weeks before made those walls ring with heart stirring eloquence.*[34]

## The Restored Government Before Congress

In addition to the pomp and circumstance observed by Congress in its opening day of special session, legislators had real business to tend, most notably hearing the Lincoln Administration's official policy regarding the seceded states.

Mr. Lincoln condemned in unmeasured terms the action of the Richmond Convention in passing an ordinance of secession, but the subsequent proceedings of the Virginia leaders, their seizure of the United States arsenal at Harper's Ferry and the navy yard at Gosport (Norfolk) he denounced even more severely. His closing words on this subject are significant:

"The people of Virginia have thus allowed this great insurrection to make its nest within her borders, and this government has no choice left but to deal with it wherever it finds it . . . and it has the less regret as the loyal citizens have in due form claimed its protection. These loyal citizens this government is bound to recognize and protect as being Virginia."[35]

### The House of Representatives

In the House of Representatives while the roll was being called, Kentucky's Virginia-born Congressman, Henry Cornelius Burnett, gave notice that he was going to move to strike from the roll of the

---

[34] Farley, Jeremy T.K., *The Civil War Out My Window* (2014).

[35] Greeley, Horace. *The American Conflict: A History of the Great Rebellion in the United States* (1865).

House the names of the five representatives from the Commonwealth of Virginia (five of Virginia's thirteen Congressmen presented themselves before the House of Representatives – having rejected their own state's secession ordinance).

These men, he declared, had been elected the preceding May, which was all right if Virginia were still in the Union, but since the state was no longer a part of the United States, the Commonwealth was no longer entitled to any representation in the United States House of Representatives.

One of the representatives explained that he had been elected regularly as prescribed by law and the only possible question which could arise was whether the ordinance for secession was to be considered valid.

Burnett's motion failed, as the House of Representatives – by this time almost entirely comprised of northern delegates – sided with the loyalist representatives from Virginia. Virginia's representatives thereupon took their seats in the House.

## The U.S. Senate

In the United States Senate, an even greater constitutional crises presented itself to federal politicians.

Wasting no time to establish themselves as the sovereign state of Virginia, the newly launched "Restored Government of Virginia" dispatched its recently appointed U.S. Senators, Carlile and Willey, to Washington in the early days of July.

Interestingly, it soon became obvious that the Wheeling government had effectively "painted themselves into a corner."

Carlile and Willey had been appointed to the Senate by a body which called itself the legislature of Virginia, but whose right to do so not many people would uphold.

Even if we were to grant the Wheeling Convention the benefit of the doubt (and this is an extremely generous gift!) and declare that they were the legal and constitutional Virginia legislature, there still remains the question of whether thirty-eight men could legally constitute an assembly in a state where the constitution required seventy-nine members present in the house of delegates and twenty-six present in the senate.

If the state could not legally secede from the Union, then its constitution was still in force and the delegates and senators sitting at

119

Wheeling could not rightfully designate themselves as the General Assembly of Virginia due to being unable to reach a legal quorum to do business.

If Virginia's secession from the Union was legal, then the state as a whole had severed its relation with the United States and the northwestern section was just as bound by this act as any other portion of the legal territory of Virginia.

Either way, there was absolutely no legal grounds justifying an assembly of random individuals, some 330-miles from the state's capitol building, lacking even a third of the total number of delegates required by law to present a quorum, to claim the necessary authority required to legally appoint senators to represent the state in the United States Senate.

The legally consistent and proper course of action the United States Senate should have taken was to declare Virginia's two senate seats "vacant," as they had already done with Alabama, Florida, Georgia, Louisiana, Mississippi, North Carolina, South Carolina, Texas, and one of Tennessee's Senate seats after their legislative bodies refused to fill the vacant seats to the federal government's upper chamber.

## A Tangled Legal Web

According to Lincoln's announced policy, none of the Confederate states had seceded because secession was unconstitutional. This being the case, the constitution of Virginia must still be in force and the General Assembly at Richmond was the only true legislative body in the state – though its members may have been guilty of treason personally, a legal legislative body could not possibly be tried for treason.

Carlile and Willey, however, presented their credentials to the body as Senators from Virginia, elected by the legislature in the ordinary manner and certified by a man who called himself Governor of Virginia.

Senator James Bayard of Delaware protested that the question of recognition involved a constitutional point which was worthy of slow deliberation and asked that the matter be referred to the Committee on Judiciary.

Maryland's senator supported this motion and said, furthermore, that at the time the Wheeling legislature had elected Carlile and Willey no vacancies existed, since Hunter and Mason had not been expelled from the Senate until the 11th of July, whereas Carlile and Willey had been elected on the 9th.

Andrew Johnson, Tennessee's loyalist senator who would become Abraham Lincoln's vice president and eventual President of the United States, stood sponsor for the two new senators from Virginia, arguing that the national legislature should accept the two men without additional questioning.

It was his opinion that the Senate should brush aside all legal questions and admit them on the evidence of their credentials. He argued that Hunter and Mason had vacated their seats long before the 9th of July and thus actual vacancies did exist.

Illinois' Republican Senator, Lyman Trumbull, said that they should not "stick in the bark" when such vital issues were presented – the new Senators were "here representing the loyal people of a disloyal state... why look beneath the surface?"

Republican Senator John P. Hale of New Hampshire was equally desirous of disregarding precedents.

Joining the chorus Unionists in the Senate, Vermont's Republican Senator, Jacob Collamer, declared that the recognition of the new government of Virginia by the President gave it legal existence as the de facto government. It was no part of the duty of the Senate to enquire into the internal affairs of a state unless called upon to do so by contesting claimants.

Retorting the men who ran to the Wheeling government's defense, Senator Bayard summed up the arguments against the admission of Carlile and Willey:

*A Senator of the United States was elected for six years and no state authority could shorten his term of office. Though elected by the legislature, he was not under its control when it came to the conduct of the office. The Senate, acting within its rights, expelled Mason and Hunter, but the legislature of Virginia, even supposing it to be a legal legislature, could not anticipate the action of the Senate, which was sole judge of the qualifications of its own members. The Executive had held that Virginia was still in the Union, since no state had the right to secede. It then followed that the state constitution was still in force;*

*Letcher was the Governor of Virginia, and any credentials presented to be valid must be signed by him.*

Those opposed to hasty action soon realized that their opposition would be to no avail – the administration had laid out a course of action regarding the seceded states and would not be swerved from that action by mere force of reason. Constitutionality must be sacrificed to expediency.

The motion to refer the case was lost five to thirty-five and the new Senators were sworn in as the successors of the Richmond government's two previous senators.

The Wheeling junta had now been officially recognized by the President and the Congress as the sovereign government of the entire Commonwealth of Virginia.

There were doubtless some persons among those sustaining the President's course who feared that a precedent might have been established which set aside the Constitution of the United States and interfered in the internal affairs of a state. But it seemed to be the general feeling, in Congress at least, that it was indeed no time to "stick in the bark." If the constitution could be preserved by liberal interpretations of its provisions, that was infinitely better than running the risk of having the Union destroyed altogether by adherence to a narrow interpretation.

To gain a foothold in Virginia would give the North a decided advantage, especially as the occupied portion was supposedly loyal to the Union.

Believing that the situation in Tennessee and North Carolina might at some time during the course of the war be similar to the circumstances presently existing in Virginia, Federal officials hoped that by showing kindness to those sympathetic to their cause others in bordering states may be inclined to act just as drastically as the rogue citizens assembled in Wheeling.

While we may sympathize with the Republican leaders in Congress in their treatment of the West Virginia question in its earlier stages, their later actions are of even more doubtful legality and are in a sense deserving of condemnation.

The recognition of the provisional government at Wheeling and the admission of West Virginia as a separate state are two very different matters.

# Debating West Virginia

The second Wheeling Convention had adjourned to meet August 6th and it soon became apparent that the only business which would occupy the attention of the adjourned meeting would be that of dividing the state.

Opposition to the new state movement had been crystallizing and the element within the Wheeling Convention which initially opposed "hasty action" on the new-state proposition now opposed it altogether.

With the Restored Government of Virginia now fully recognized by the federal government's executive and legislative branches, many of the delegates who had attended the first two Wheeling Conventions began having second thoughts as to the necessity of forming a second state altogether.

Evidence of this can be found in an editorial piece published in *The Wheeling Intelligencer* in which an impatient writer made the accusation that the officers of the reorganized state were working against the setting-up of a state separate from Virginia.

On July 22, 1861, the Wheeling body, calling itself the "Virginia House of Delegates," met and debated authorizing the "Western Counties" to break from Virginia and form a new state.

## West Virginia: The Desire of Northern Federal Politicians

Despite the opposition of a handful of honest constitutionalists in Congress, most of the northern politicians serving in the Federal government's House and Senate looked favorably upon the division of Virginia, the capital of the Southern Confederacy.

By dividing the South's crown jewel, the legislative powers in Washington hoped to deal a death blow to the seceded Richmond government and thus end the American Civil War as quickly as possible.

Sensing the favorable political climate in the nation's capital, one that had never previously existed, the same northwestern Virginia politicians who had been advocating for a new state for decades past, seized the opportunity to move forward with their fraudulent plan – even in the face of growing opposition among a substantial number of residents from the proposed new state's central and southern regions.

Undeterred by overwhelming public opposition, the "representatives" serving within the Restored Government's "General Assembly" introduced an act which, if passed, would give the August Wheeling Convention the power to erect a new state, providing certain boundaries were adhered to.

It was further stipulated that provision should be made for the assumption by the new state of a share of the state debt contracted before May 23, 1861, and that other counties not included in the original draft should be permitted to vote on the question of uniting with their sister counties of the west.

The original boundary of the new state was to run from the Tug Fork of the Big Sandy River on the Kentucky border to the dividing line between Buchannan and Logan counties; then from the dividing line between Wyoming and McDowell to the Great Flat Mountains along the boundaries of Raleigh, Mercer, Fayette, Nicholas, Greenbrier, Webster, Pocahontas, Randolph, Pendleton, and Highland counties to the Shenandoah Mountains.

The line then ran between the counties of Pendleton and Rockingham, Hardy and Shenandoah, Hampshire and Frederick, Morgan and Berkeley to the state line of Maryland.

The convention was to make necessary arrangements for drawing up a constitution which should be submitted to the people of the proposed state.

Even with its initial borders leaving out several secessionist counties which would eventually be brought into the fold, it was a commonly accepted fact that a large portion of the proposed new state's territory included significant sections that had no desire to leave the Commonwealth, nor side with the Pierpont government.

MAP: One of several proposed boundaries for the State of Kanawha.

124

Proof of this can be found in a letter to the editor published in the *Wheeling Intelligencer.*

"The editor of this paper argued against the inclusion of known Secessionist counties. 'If their people are hostile, the new state would perhaps be worth more without than with them. . . . Coercion is necessary in suppressing a rebellion, but forcing people into a new government is not suppressing rebellion.'"[36]

## The Objection of Western Virginia Representatives

Delegate James West of Wetzel County, who had hitherto been at the forefront of the West Virginia advocates, disclosed the fact that he had undergone a change in opinion.

He declared that the people of Western Virginia were changing their minds in the matter of cutting loose from the Commonwealth and now there was grave doubt if the majority in any county was in favor of separation.

This view was sustained by another member, who was frank enough to admit that he was in doubt as to whether or not their body could legally even give its consent to the formation of a new state.

Passing by the legal question, there was still remaining the question regarding whether a new state was even necessary or best for the parties involved.

Not more than one-fifth of the people of Virginia were represented and not more than one-half of the one-fifth of residents desired the division of the state.

One of the advocates of separation, Joseph Snyder of Monongalia County, retorted that if he represented no more of a constituency than did some of the other gentlemen on the floor he could sit down and write to every one of them in fifteen minutes asking their opinion on the point under discussion.

The people who had sent him desired immediate separation, he stated, "if the present legislature could do one thing it could do another."

Delegate Snyder closed with the accusation that some of the members had been "bought."

---

[36] July 22, 1861. *Wheeling Intelligencer.*

No further action was taken at this session and the legislature adjourned July 26th.

## August 1861: The Third Wheeling Convention

On August 6th the third meeting of the Wheeling Convention reassembled. Delegates from thirty-one counties[37] were present.

After the preliminary business had been disposed of, a committee consisting of one member from each county represented was appointed to take up the questions of the division of the state and the confiscation of rebel property.

Farnsworth, another new-state man, astonished the convention by making a motion to adjourn *sine die* (without assigning a day for a further meeting or hearing, basically ending the convention indefinitely).

The legislature, he said, had gone on record as opposed to the division of the state and nothing could be done without its consent.

Farnsworth's motion failed and the delegates continued in their effort to carve up the map.

A resolution was offered providing for the formation of a new state from the Tennessee line to the top of the Alleghany Mountains to the Maryland border.

Carlile, whose prestige was

MAP: One of several proposals made by the "large state" advocates.

---

[37] The counties represented were Hancock, Ohio, Brooke, Marshall, Wetzel, Marion, Monongalia, Wayne, Mason, Jackson, Wood, Tyler, Doddridge, Pleasants, Ritchie, Jefferson, Taylor, Hardy, Preston, Fairfax, Tucker, Hampshire, Randolph, Kanawha, Barbour, Wirt, Upshur, Harrison, Gilmer, and Lewis. The town of Alexandria was represented by Gilbert Miner.

enhanced by his senatorial toga, took the position that it would be a mistake to include any county where the people were opposed to a division.

Under the provision of the above proposal, a number of counties would become part of a state with which they were entirely out of sympathy. Far better would it be to make the new state smaller and more united in opinion, he argued.

His views were embodied in a resolution presented August 9, 1861, whereby the new state should consist of thirty-eight counties all lying west of the Alleghenies. Any county contiguous to the enumerated counties could by a popular vote annex itself to the new state.

Carlile's views were endorsed by the *Wheeling Intelligencer*, which declared that a voluntary association of thirty counties was far better than an association of sixty unwilling counties.

## Silencing the Will of the Voters

Realizing just how unpopular the prospect of West Virginia statehood would be to the vast majority of citizens affected, most delegates who favored the creation of a new state were opposed to any scheme which included the taking of a vote of the people.

The legislature and the convention, said Chapman J. Stewart of Doddridge County, were for all practical purposes "the people" and if they had gone thus far with no popular sanction they could proceed just as far as was necessary in order to carry out their plan.

He challenged any person to point to a solitary act that had even authorized them to assemble for the purpose of breaking away from Virginia.

It was true that this idea had been in the minds of many people, but no one present could present instructions from his constituents urging him to work for separation. As for himself, he did not believe the matter had ever been thought of by the people who elected him. If the convention was resolved to form a new state, let it do so without the inconvenience of a popular election.

The ordinance presented by the Committee on Division showed that the large-state advocates had triumphed in the committee. The boundary line was to be drawn from the Tennessee line through the valley of Virginia to the boundary between Frederick County and Prince William County on the Potomac River. One commentator wrote, "A more arbitrary line of division could scarcely have been conceived."

No real natural boundaries existed between the proposed new state and old Virginia under the ordinance outlined. To safeguard against certain rejection in at least two-thirds of the counties, the vote was to be taken as a whole, no county being allowed to vote as a unit. This would ensure the acceptance of the plan, for it was well understood that in few counties outside the northern Panhandle would the people take the matter seriously enough to vote even where a poll was permitted.

The Secessionists controlled all but a few of the counties, and it was unthinkable that they would permit a vote to be taken in those counties.

The delegates favoring the above plan were opportunists.

It was felt that a little further stretching of the constitution and a little more disregard of popular opinion would do no harm, especially as they had the assurance that their actions would be sustained by the Federal Government.

The chance to break away from Virginia might never come again and western Virginia would be compelled to endure indefinitely the imagined oppression of the East.

The leader of the group of politicians known as the "opportunists," those who favored seizing the moment to create a large state, was Wetzel County's Mr. West.

West favored taking in the central and extreme southern Virginia counties whether they wished it or not and declared his opposition to any plan which did not include a large number of counties.

The ordinance under consideration suited him, he said, "because it contained the grave of Washington."

Congress undoubtedly had the power to admit the proposed new state, but to do so it would have to disregard constitutions and establish precedents and recognize, virtually, an act of secession.

### *Not a mandate by any means*

On August 14, 1861, Daniel Farnsworth brought in a substitute to the committee's plan.

He proposed to make the Alleghenies the eastern boundary of the state, thus excluding those counties which were known to be in open sympathy with the Southern cause.

Arthur Boreman of Tyler County urged that it would be premature to take any action at this time since the counties were in such a disturbed condition that a full, free vote was impossible.

Delegate Andrew Ritchie took the position that the convention was exceeding its powers and instructions in even considering a division of the old state at this time. It had been called to reorganize the government of Virginia, an act which had been accomplished.

Further proceedings would embarrass the general government and start a discussion of the slavery question.

To enforce his views, Delegate Ritchie read a letter from Attorney General Edward Bates who said that he had talked over the situation in Western Virginia with a number of officials and all agreed that the division of Virginia would be an original act of revolution.

This opinion was concurred by many who were not opponents of division per se, but who doubted the expediency of the action under existing conditions.

No one seriously believed, they said, that division could be accomplished constitutionally while Virginia was in rebellion against the Federal Government, and to attempt it would present the Lincoln Administration with yet another challenging problem to solve. More than this, it would be a cowardly act to desert the tiny minority of Union men in the eastern counties.

While not constituting a majority in any county, the number of loyal citizens in eastern Virginia was sufficiently large enough to deserve consideration. As for the state debt, there was no honorable way whereby the proposed new state could be relieved from the necessity of saddling itself with a heavy burden. If repudiation were attempted, the bondholders would check any further progress of the movement in Congress.

Lieutenant Governor Polsley spoke in opposition to division. With the example of the Richmond Convention before them, they should take warning and limit themselves to the consideration of the questions which they had been called together to settle.

Unlike Virginia's secession from the Union, which was put to popular vote, all knew that if the ardent new-state men had their way, no such vote would be allowed leading up to Western Virginia's secession from Virginia – under existing conditions not one-fourth of the counties could or would vote.

Even the representative from the northern panhandle's Ohio County, Chester D. Hubbard, agreed that it would be selfish to consider local interests while the United States Government was in such grave peril. All loyal Western Virginians should be willing to remain in the old state just as long as they could thereby benefit the Federal government.

Senator Carlile, in answer to this, denied that the administration would be embarrassed in any way by being called upon to decide the status of the western counties. As for local sentiment, if they waited for a full representation from every county the state would never be formed. Interest was the base of all political action and was justification enough for their purpose.

Daniel Lamb of Ohio County presented the case of the opposition in its clearest form. He was in favor of division just as soon as it could be accomplished in the proper manner, when a full and free expression of opinion could be obtained.

It had been less than two months since the reorganized government had been set up and already there were many who were not satisfied. Such haste seemed suspicious in view of the fact that there was now no danger threatening them.

Delegate Lamb was proceeding on the assumption that the reorganized government would go out of existence when the new state was admitted. He thought that after the Federal authorities had taken possession of the eastern part of the state, it would be necessary to set up a government there and a clash between the two sets of officials in Virginia was inevitable.

It is evident that Lamb was ignorant of the fact that there was no intention to do away with the provisional government.

Carlile now proposed a compromise, which provided for the inclusion of the counties under the Farnsworth plan and the submission of the question to the counties individually. An amendment to this was adopted, substituting the boundaries of the original committee recommendation.

## Setting the Boundaries

On Monday, August, 19, 1861, a new committee of six was appointed to agree upon some compromise measure.

The ordinance presented by them on the following day became the one upon which the present State of West Virginia was founded.

Thirty-nine counties were to be included and the new state's proposed name was Kanawha.

## Fair Elections?

The committee stated that an election should be held on October 24, 1861, at which delegates were to be chosen to a constitutional convention and at the same time the people of Greenbrier, Pocahontas, Hardy, Hampshire, Morgan, Berkeley, and Jefferson counties were to be permitted to vote on the question of annexation to the new state.

The sections of the ordinance providing for the holding of the election contained some curious features:

One of sections stated that if the county officials refused to open the polls, any two freemen could do so anywhere in the county and constitute themselves the election commissioners. The possibilities of fraud in an election conducted after this manner are too evident to require comment.

## Debating West Virginia

The state was to assume a fair proportion of that part of the Virginia debt which had been created prior to January 1, 1861.

P.G. Van Winkle in supporting the report, of the committee explained that he himself was a recent convert to the small state plan, having been brought to see that it would be unwise to include any portion of the Valley where the people were so strongly in favor of secession.

Those favoring the large state were dissatisfied with the committee's report as were, of course, the opponents of separation under any circumstances.

Neither of these factions could be brought to see that the inclusion of the Valley counties was desirable at all, although they admitted that there was some truth in the statement that the feeling against separation in some of the counties taken in by the committee's plan was no less strong than that in the counties east of the Alleghenies.

Delegate Campbell Tarr succeeded in having passed a motion to include Hampshire, Hardy, Morgan, Berkeley, and Jefferson counties unconditionally.

Its adoption gave rise to a bitter discussion.

Carlile asserted that the people of these counties would be denied any choice in the matter. Hampshire and Jefferson had even voted in favor of the ratification of the ordinance of secession, and there was every reason for believing that the pro-Southern feeling was stronger now. The thirty-nine counties first included in the committee report contained few slaves, but this number would be raised by eight thousand if the resolution just adopted was not rejected.

MAP of Hampshire, Hardy, Morgan, Berkeley and Jefferson Counties – as they were in 1861.

By this time, Carlile had reached the opinion that "the only West Virginia was northwestern Virginia. The remainder of the section west of the mountains was in total sympathy with the east. The two western divisions of Virginia had little in common." He adds that he was surprised to find in Wheeling a strong sentiment against the division of the state.

Carlile's views prevailed and Tarr's motion was reconsidered and voted down.

The ordinance was then adopted, fifty to twenty-eight. A number of the members voting aye explained and apologized for their action, saying that their only reason for agreeing to the ordinance was the conviction that it was the best that could be obtained at the time.

The business of the convention was now over and it adjourned to meet at the call of the Governor or of the presiding officer, if such a call should be made before the first Thursday of January 1862. After that time the convention was to go out of existence automatically.

# Chapter Nine

# The Civil War
# in Western Virginia

The Federal recruiting officers found it difficult to raise troops anywhere in Virginia, even in the supposedly loyal northwestern counties. The people of the West preferred being left alone by both contending parties, but it was especially repugnant to them to be pitted in battle against their own fellow-citizens of Virginia.

In Wheeling, by May 23, 1861, there were five hundred and forty-one soldiers in camp and the officers reported to the *Pittsburgh Chronicle* that the work of raising troops was a slow process.

During this same time, large numbers of Southern troops gathered in Clarksburg, Fairmont and Grafton and remained until the arrival of a Union army sent them into retreat.

It was reported that on May 22, 1861, there were a thousand Secessionists at Clarksburg, three thousand at Grafton and one thousand at Fairmont.

On June 10th, thirty-two Confederate sympathizers left the city for Harper's Ferry, vowing never to return until "the Goths and Vandals had been driven out."

Later in the summer, a correspondent of the *Indianapolis Journal* wrote that while West Virginia was said to have three regiments in the field, out of one thousand men, only one hundred and fifty were from Virginia, the remainder being from western Pennsylvania and eastern Ohio.

This was true of all the regiments. "You will see lying around country towns scores of great big, ugly, awkward, stand-up-and-call-your mother- a-liar fellows who are Virginians, but not in the army," remarked one Northern commentator.[38]

At the very least one half of the people in western Virginia were out-and-out Secessionists.

*The Cincinnati Gazette* expressed its disappointment at the evident apathy of West Virginia in the matter of enlisting in the Union army. It declared that there was good reason to suppose that the attachment of the section to the Union was not as strong as had been supposed.

An editorial in the *Wellsburg Herald*, Aug. 3, takes the Western Virginians severely to task for their reluctance to enlist in the Union army. Referring to the fact that most of the troops guarding the section were from Ohio and Pennsylvania, the editor says: "We would not be surprised if the patriotic Ohioans would have such a high opinion of the amiability of their Virginia brethren of the Union persuasion that they may be induced to settle down and become a permanent guard over their lives and property. A pretty condition Northwestern Virginia is in to establish herself into a separate state... after all the drumming and all the gas about a separate state she has actually organized in the field four not entire regiments of soldiers and one of these hails almost entirely from the Panhandle. In a white population of over a quarter of a million, 3,000 men to stand up for the Union is truly a heavy draft upon the patriotism of our section."

The editor of the *Wheeling Intelligencer*, Aug. 13th, stated authoritatively that there were in Western Virginia 14 regiments of Ohio volunteers, 3 of Indiana, 2 of Kentucky, 3 of Virginia, two of the latter being part full.

---

[38] *Wheeling Intelligencer*, Aug. 10, 1861.

It may be stated with some degree of certainty that the false impressions which had gotten out regarding the Union feeling in West Virginia were a direct result of the articles appearing in newspapers like the *Wheeling Intelligencer* in which the wish was father to the thought.

In professing to speak for the whole western region, the *Wheeling Intelligencer* persuaded the North that West Virginia was thoroughly loyal and would respond unflinchingly at the call of the Federal Government.

The discovery was soon made, however, that the loyalty of the people was in inverse proportion to their distance from the Northern states. If correspondents in Wheeling were convinced that the people of the northern Panhandle were indifferent what would they expect to find in the interior counties, where the danger of Yankee invasion was comparatively small?

Just as the large body of Western Virginians were neutral in the conflict that was pending, so were they indifferent as to the actions of the Wheeling government, showing their disapproval by staying away from the polls. There was a general feeling that the new state if formed would be the result of a secret, restless desire on the part of aspiring politicians to obtain offices.

## Letters of the Day vs. Newspaper Reports

As is often the case in contemporary America, the agenda driven news media of the day was far more interested in pushing their own private objectives than actually providing readers with an honest account of the current events.

Consequently, the student of history will quickly discover that the private correspondences between policy makers differ wildly from the Civil War accounts of the nationwide Union media.

Letter from Ironton, Ohio,
Nov. 2, 1861, to Adjutant General Samuels:
*"The provisional government of Virginia seems to be more popular with a majority of our people than our own state government, for we have only about two hundred men from this county enlisted in Ohio regiments."*

The writer stated that there were eleven full companies from his county enlisted "as Virginians."

Letter to General Samuels,
Kanawha Court House, April 14, 1862:
*"Almost all the old officers are rebels. . . . How are we to deal with Secessionists? . . . Please understand we are just about as though the Regiment had never been organized."*

Letter to Governor Pierpont
From Fairmont, March 10, 1862,
Signed John Google, Company I, 18th Regiment:
*"They had elected a most vile Secessionist as Captain. A majority are rebels and would like nothing better than to hand over the organization to the South."*

Letter to Governor Pierpont
From Colonel Harris,
10th Regiment, located at Harrisville, March 27, 1862:
*"The election of officers in the Gilmer County Company was a farce. The men elected were rebels and bush-whackers. The election of these men was intended, no doubt, as a burlesque on the reorganization of the militia."*

Letter to General Samuels
From Captain Hall
Glenville, Gilmer County, March 19, 1862:
*"The election of officers resulted in a perfect burlesque. They were all secession leaders of guerrilla parties."*

## West Virginia: The Creation of Opportunistic Politicians

Under the old regime, West Virginia had fared badly in the distribution of state offices (particularly prior to the Constitution of 1851), but it must be admitted that the west had produced few able men.

In 1860 Carlile, Boreman, Pierpont, and Willey were only local celebrities.

The same group of men who organized the May convention and summoned the June convention, called together and sat as members of the rump legislature; meeting one day as a convention, passing an ordinance setting up a new state; the same men returned the following day as the General Assembly of Virginia and gave their consent to the very act which they had agreed to the previous day; creating offices for themselves and fixing their own salaries.

Then, to cap the climax, a free vote was made impossible and no one but known adherents of the new state were permitted to go to the polls. It was admitted that even in the Panhandle there was no enthusiasm for the new state.

In June 1861, George McC. Porter attempted to arouse the spirit of a Wheeling audience by asserting that he was "born in Virginia and hope[d] to die in West Virginia."[39]

Instead of being applauded, the statement was received with silence. As strange as it may seem, when the much-longed-for opportunity arrived, the people of West Virginia discovered that their Virginia pride was far stronger than they had imagined.

### Back in Richmond

Across the mountains, Richmond observed the progress of affairs in northwestern Virginia with mingled anger and alarm.

In his message to the Virginia Assembly, December 2, 1861, Governor Letcher denounced the unpatriotic spirit exhibited by a portion of the people in the northwest and characterized their acts aimed at the dismemberment of the state as disloyal and revolutionary. Their conduct, said the Governor, was without justification or excuse, especially as their leaders had pledged themselves to abide by and acquiesce in this popular expression of sentiment.

---

[39] *Wheeling Intelligencer*, July 1, 1861.

*"But instead of this they had given aid to an army composed of the reckless and the abandoned, the dissolute and the depraved, gathered from the purlieus of the cities and villages of the north and the floating scum of western population."*

The section should not be abandoned to the traitor residents and the mercenary soldiery, said Governor Letcher. Many loyal Virginians had been driven from their homes while their property was confiscated; it was the sacred duty of the state to repossess them of their lost goods.

"The commonwealth must not be dismembered. When the war ends she must be what she was when it was inaugurated. The Ohio River was the western boundary then and it must continue to be her boundary," stated the Virginia Governor.

On June 14, 1861, Governor Letcher had issued a proclamation to the people of northwestern Virginia, informing them that the state had ratified the ordinance of secession by a majority of nearly 100,000, imploring local residents, "Men of the northwest, I appeal to you by all the considerations which have drawn us together as one people heretofore to rally to the standard of the Old Dominion. By all the sacred ties of consanguinity ... by memories of the past, by the relics of the great men of other days, come to Virginia's banner and drive the invaders from your soil. There may be traitors in the midst of you who, for selfish ends, have turned against their mother and would permit her to be ignominiously oppressed and degraded. But I cannot, will not, believe that a majority of you are not true sons who will give your blood and your treasure for Virginia's defense."

Eastern Virginia had only the vaguest notion of what was taking place in the western portion of the state. Refugees brought wild stories of the acts of cruelty and oppression perpetrated by the Union men. But for the presence of Union troops, it was asserted, the whole country would be aroused for secession.

*Wild Rumors*

As is often the case with events of this magnitude, the absurdity of reality lent itself to wild and outrageous rumors.

No rumor was too absurd to obtain credence.

It was commonly reported that the Pierpont government had passed an ordinance divorcing all refugee husbands from their wives, declaring that no citizen of Virginia could remain in lawful matrimony with a citizen of the restored state, but that the mere act of flight from the loyal counties to the seceded portion of the state dissolved the marriage tie.

According to one writer, newspapers not in sympathy with the prosecution of the war were not allowed to circulate in the part of West Virginia under Federal supervision – as a matter of fact, the very reverse was true. *The Wheeling Intelligencer*, as strong a Union paper as there was in the United States, was not allowed circulation in most of the western counties by the action of the citizens themselves – as they viewed the newspaper to be too extreme and treasonous against the Old Dominion.[40]

It was a common belief that the only Union sympathizers in West Virginia were foreigners and recent settlers from free states. "The native West Virginians, with a few dishonorable exceptions, are true to the South," one paper stated. This impression was confirmed by all the refugees from Western Virginia who exaggerated the number of Secessionists as much as possible.

# A Losing Battle

As the success of the Southern cause in West Virginia became less probable, the bitterness of the East increased.

Letcher found his chief diversion in railing against the Pierpont government. Indicting Lincoln for permitting Pierpont to plunder the state treasury of $40,000, for subjecting Virginia to the jurisdiction of foreign laws, for quartering large bodies of troops in the state, etc.

The report of the United States Secretary of War in December, 1861, awakened great resentment in Virginia.

### A Plan to Divide Virginia Even Further

Simon Cameron, Lincoln's Secretary of War, recommended the reconstruction of Maryland, Delaware, and Virginia, with the purpose in view of making the city of Washington less accessible to attack.

He suggested that the boundary of Virginia should be altered, so that she would be shut in on the north and east by Pennsylvania and the Blue Ridge Mountains.

---

[40] *Richmond Whig.* August 10, 1861.

Two counties of Maryland were to be annexed to Virginia, and all of the state lying between the Blue Ridge and Chesapeake Bay was to become part of Maryland. A portion of the peninsula between Chesapeake Bay and the Atlantic Ocean, held by Virginia and Maryland, was to be incorporated into Delaware.

Finally, it was urged that the part of the District of Columbia retroceded to Virginia should be taken back.

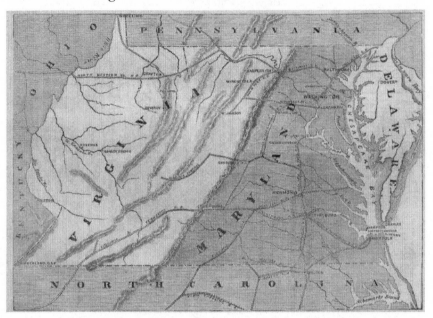

MAP appearing in *Harper's Weekly* on December 21, 1861, p. 806 with the following footnote: "Map showing the new boundaries of Virginia, Maryland, and Delaware as proposed by Secretary Cameron."

To this the *Richmond Dispatch* responded:

*"There can be no Virginia unless it includes both eastern and western Virginia. Cameron, the execrable Secretary of War of the Lincoln despotism, has presented the servile Congress of that loathsome tyranny with a map in which eastern Virginia is attached to Maryland. . . . We say that if we cannot hold West Virginia we can hardly defend the South."*

January, 1862, the General Assembly at Richmond passed a joint resolution subject of the division of the state. It read as follows:

*"Whereas the public enemy, invited by domestic foes, being in power within some of the counties in Virginia, where they are confiscating the property of loyal citizens and otherwise oppressing them in a cruel manner; and whereas the traitors there, contemplating a division of this time-honored commonwealth with the aid of this public enemy have set up a pretended government over the same, which under the force of circumstances could not be prevented by the timely sending of an adequate military force; and whereas the legislature desires to reassure all loyal citizens throughout the commonwealth of their desire and intention to protect them, therefore, Resolved by the Senate and House of Delegates that in no event will the state of Virginia submit to or consent to the loss of a foot of her soil; that it is the firm determination of the state... to assert and maintain the jurisdiction and sovereignty of Virginia to the utmost limits of her ancient boundaries at any and every cost."*

There was a noticeable indisposition on the part of the authorities of Virginia to pass retaliatory acts against the western section.

Pierpont and his colleagues were excoriated in the severest terms, but it was thoroughly believed that the great mass of people disapproved of the Wheeling government, and therefore should not be punished for something which was more their misfortune than their fault.

## "The People" Vote for West Virginia

October 21, 1861, was the day designated by the Wheeling government for the vote on the question of dividing the state and the election of delegates to the constitutional convention.

Few people beyond the borders of the northwestern counties took the slightest interest in the affair, although the editors of the loyal newspapers did their best to arouse the people to the importance of the occasion.

The editor of the *Wheeling Intelligencer* devoted many columns in his efforts to awaken the citizens from their apathy which, he predicted, would prevent West Virginia from becoming a reality.

What the people really needed, he said, was a more intense love for the Union and a greater hatred of secession.

In many of the western counties rebel soldiers had returned to their homes and were living there undisturbed by their loyal neighbors.

"Moreover, it was safer to be a Secessionist in these counties than to be known as a Northern supporter, for the latter as a class had no pluck or stamina."
- Wheeling Intelligencer, Oct. 15, 1861.

The correspondent of the *Cincinnati Commercial* wrote:
"The most curious, miserly set of beings I ever saw are the Union men of West Virginia. I have never seen but one who would expend a dime towards the preservation of the Union."

### A Manipulated Election

It was well understood that there would be almost no votes cast on the question of division outside the northwest, and the necessity was plain of rolling up as large a majority for separation as possible.

Instead of allowing a free vote, the election was so manipulated that it was difficult for the opponents of the ordinance to register their protests.

As a result, the vote proves too much.

We have presented evidence showing the strength of secession in all portions of West Virginia.

What then is to be inferred when we find the official vote reported as follows:

Putnam County, 209 for, none against division;
Cabell, 200 to nothing;
Gilmer, unanimous (no vote given);
Clay, 96 to 0;

142

Raleigh, 32 to 0;
Harrison, 1,148 to 2;
Marion, 760 to 38;
Monongalia, 1,591 to 18;
Upshur, 614 to 0;
Randolph, 171 to 2, etc.

The official vote was announced to be 18,408 for division and 781 against it.

This is interesting considering the fact that the West Virginia Department of Archives and History believes that Confederate and Union numbers were about equal (22,000-25,000).[41]
The student of history should also find it extraordinarily curious that in addition to being home to +20,000 Confederate soldiers, voters in what would become the State of West Virginia voted by a margin of 48,647 to 1,402 against Abraham Lincoln in November 1860... The following May, 3,076 voters from just three West Virginia counties (Mercer, Monroe and Greenbrier) voted to secede from the Union and join the Confederate States of America... yet when it came time to vote on whether the Commonwealth of Virginia should be divided and have its spoils presented as a gift to the Federal government, only 781 individuals came out in opposition?

No thinking person can view the West Virginia Statehood popular vote – in light of the Presidential Election of 1860, the Virginia Secession Ordinance of May 1861, and the number of Confederate soldiers from the Mountain State and truly believe that this was a fair and accurate election.

In reality, one can only conclude that the election was riddled with fraud, poorly advertised (by design), or a combination of the two.

*Voter Suppression:*
The newspapers of the day hint at the methods used to exclude voters: *The Ritchie County Democrat*, for example, suggested that no one should be allowed to vote but known Union men.

It is more than doubtful if 18,000 votes were cast altogether.

---

[41] "The Civil War in West Virginia." www.wvculture.org. Web. 20 September 2015.

The whole matter was treated with derision and contempt in the southern and eastern counties – described by Union writers as "the wilderness of secession," one cannot imagine that election notices were posted and the polls opened October 24th, as was provided for in the ordinance.

When it is remembered that by this vote the counties of the new state were supposed to express their approval of a division of Virginia and of the appeal to Congress to admit them as a new state, the dishonest nature of West Virginia's origin may be fully perceived.

## Stonewall Jackson
## West Virginia's Confederate General

Since 1984, all government offices in the Commonwealth of Virginia have closed their doors on the Friday preceding the third Monday of January. The Old Dominion celebrates a statewide holiday honoring Confederate General Thomas Jonathan Jackson – the holiday is known as Lee-Jackson Day.

Though the Virginia government in Richmond proudly claims him as their own – as they should – most in modern-day Virginia and even West Virginia are shocked to learn that the famed rebel commander actually hails from what is now Clarksburg, West Virginia.

"But how could this be?" I was once asked by a young and dumbfounded collegiate, who went on to state, "I thought that West Virginians sided with the North during the Civil War?"

Unfortunately, this total lack of understanding when it comes to history seems to have permeated itself into the psyche of modern-day Americans, so much so that what the average American now thinks he or she knows about history is mostly erroneous – especially when it comes to the Civil War and the creation of West Virginia in particular.

In reality, unlike most of the other southern generals serving in the American Civil War, General Jackson was engaged in a battle for his state's very existence.

Recognizing the fact that forces outside of their counties, regions and even state were attempting to subvert their will and decapitate their native homeland, men like Jackson and thousands of others from the Western Virginia mountains answered Richmond's call to battle.

Among the thousands of West Virginians who answered this call to defend the Richmond government was my great-great-great grandfather, Thomas Benton Farley, a native of Logan County, Virginia.

Fueled by the understanding that defeat on the battlefield equated directly to no longer being a Virginian, a title nearly all of the settlers of southern West Virginia bore proudly, Jackson and his band of soldiers, including my grandfather, stood out in battle.

On July 21, 1861, the valor of Jackson and his fighting Virginians, many of which were Western Virgnians, would forever be etched into the American lore as the warriors stood fearlessly in defense of the Commonwealth against an invading Union army.

With Confederate lines crumbling all around them under a heavy Northern assault, Jackson's brigade stood unyielding, a testament to their discipline and determination to defend their Virginia at all costs.

Observing their commitment to the fight, South Carolina's commander exhorted his own troops to rejoin the battle by shouting, "There is Jackson standing like a stone wall. Let us determine to die here, and we will conquer. Rally behind the Virginians!"

Only moments after rallying his soldiers behind the Virginians, the Palmetto State's brigadier general who coined the enduring title for Jackson would be killed in battle; nevertheless, Jackson's brigade, which would thenceforth be known as the "Stonewall Brigade," stopped the Union assault, resiliently suffering more casualties than any other Southern brigade that day.

Jackson, a devoutly religious man who was known for possessing an extreme view of predestination, would often hold his left arm skyward with the palm facing forward – apparently as part of his routine battle-prayer, requesting success in combat before the Almighty.

A few months after his success at Bull Run, while holding his arm up in battle, part of Jackson's finger was shot off. Against the will of his doctors, the Western Virginian refused to have his finger amputated.

In the days ahead, Jackson would be promoted to major general and serve gallantly throughout the remainder of the war.

As commander of the Virginia Valley District, Jackson defended the heart of the Commonwealth against attacking Union forces intent upon taking the Confederate capital at Richmond.

One commentator writes, "Jackson possessed the attributes to succeed against his poorly coordinated and sometimes timid opponents: a combination of great audacity, excellent knowledge and shrewd use of the terrain, and the ability to inspire his troops to great feats of marching and fighting."[42]

Despite being outnumbered, the Tygart Valley native racked up numerous victories throughout 1862, defeating advancing Union forces throughout the entire state – seeing triumphs from the Blue Ridge Mountains of Rockingham County to the eastern shore at Hanover County.

The successes of Jackson and his soldiers of Western Virginia proved to be a cause of concern for Lincoln and the Northern Army – Jackson and his men were known to be the most fierce and steadfast soldiers to have served during the Civil War.

Unfortunately for the cause of Virginia, Jackson's tenure as the great defender of the Commonwealth would be short lived, as his life was abruptly ended during the Battle of Chancellorsville in the spring of 1863.

In a strange twist of fate, the brave and fearless Confederate general would not be killed during actual battle, but instead lose his life due to events which occurred just hours after having outflanked an entire Union army – a maneuver that resulted in the capture of scores of northern soldiers and valuable caches of ammunition.

With evening now spent, Jackson and his entourage were returning on horseback to the Confederate headquarters along the same turnpike they had traveled earlier that afternoon.

As they journeyed, the group of Virginia soldiers spooked the 18th North Carolina Infantry Regiment who were standing guard along the road.

The Carolina soldiers shouted, "Halt, who goes there?"

Before Jackson and his men were given an opportunity to identify themselves, the Tarheeled militia fired into the darkness.

---

[42] "Stonewall Jackson." Wikipedia. 20 September 2015. Web. 20 September 2015.

Frantic shouts by Jackson's staff identifying the party were replied to by Major John D. Barry with the retort, "It's a damned Yankee trick! Fire!"

With no fewer than two volleys being hurled into the darkness, several of Jackson's men were killed and the general himself was hit by three bullets – two in the left arm and one in the right hand.

Jackson's men raced to place him on a stretcher and remove him from danger, however, incoming rounds of artillery caused the Western Virginian to be dropped from the stretcher and suffer additional injuries.

In the days ahead, Jackson's injuries would be compounded by pneumonia.

Having grown deathly ill in a week's time, Jackson awoke on the morning of Sunday, May 10, 1863, and remarked, "It is the Lord's Day; my wish is fulfilled. I have always desired to die on Sunday."

Dr. McGuire wrote an account of the general's final hours and his last words:

"A few moments before he died he cried out in his delirium, 'Order A.P. Hill to prepare for action! Pass the infantry to the front rapidly! Tell Major Hawks'—then stopped, leaving the sentence unfinished. Presently a smile of ineffable sweetness spread itself over his pale face, and he said quietly, and with an expression, as if of relief, 'Let us cross over the river, and rest under the shade of the trees'; and then without pain or the least struggle, his spirit passed from earth to the God who gave it."[43]

The night General Robert E. Lee learned of Jackson's death, he told his cook, "William, I have lost my right arm... I'm bleeding at the heart."

*Harpers Weekly* reported Jackson's death on May 23, 1863, as follows:

## DEATH OF STONEWALL JACKSON.

*General "Stonewall" Jackson was badly wounded in the arm at the battles of Chancellorsville, and had his arm amputated. The*

---

[43] *Southern Historical Society Papers*, Volumes 13-14. (1886) p. 162-163.

*operation did not succeed, and pneumonia setting in, he died on the 10th inst., near Richmond, Virginia.*

Though no one in the South dared to admit it, news of Jackson's death signaled the end for the Southern cause.

The final outcome of the War Between the States had already been decided, the remaining question would be at what expense.

According to the 1923 book, *The History of West Virginia, Old and New,* my great-great-great grandfather, Thomas Benton Farley, was with the general "at the time when that intrepid officer met his death..."

Like so many others from Western Virginia, Farley, the young man from Logan County who had taken part in so many great victories under General Jackson would spend the remaining days of the war in great misery.

Just weeks following Jackson's death, my 3x great-grandfather would be captured by Union forces and transported to Point Lookout Federal Prison Camp in Maryland.

Although the Union prison camp was originally constructed to house only 10,000 men, as the war drug on, the number of prisoners housed at the complex would swell to over 50,000 incarcerated soldiers. According to the Maryland Department of Natural Resources, nearly 4,000 of these prisoners of war died – a result of atrociously unsanitary conditions, starvation, overcrowding (sixteen men to a small tent) and other unspeakable atrocities.

In 1861, my great-grandfather's grandfather joined the fight for Virginia's defense just months after having married Nancy Pinson, daughter of a prominent citizen of Pike County, Kentucky.

He was held as a prisoner of war until 1865 – a captive of Northern forces who had successfully changed the state government of his home community, against his will and the will of nearly everyone else in the County of Logan.

# Chapter Ten

# Creating West Virginia's First Constitution

On November 26, 1861, delegates to the Constitutional Convention gathered in Wheeling in order to frame a constitution for the proposed State of Kanawha.

Interestingly, only thirty-seven of the seventy-five elected delegates were present, representing thirty-one counties: Randolph, Tucker, Preston, Marion, Taylor, Barbour, Upshur, Harrison, Lewis, Kanawha, Wayne, Cabell, Putnam, Mason, Jackson, Roane, Wirt, Gilmer, Ritchie, Wood, Pleasants, Tyler, Doddridge, Wetzel, Marshall, Hancock, Ohio, Hampshire, Hardy, Boone and Brooke.

Absolutely no election returns were reported from Logan, Nicholas, Webster, Calhoun, Wyoming and Fayette.

Before the convention was formally organized, a contest arose over the representation of Wyoming and Fayette counties, which had not held elections, "owing to the hostile state of the county."

Though an undeniable majority of the residents of these counties did not approve of a separation from Virginia, a handful of men appeared in Wheeling claiming to be the delegates of these counties.

Though they had not been elected by the people through a legal election, they presented signed petitions by supposed residents of the counties as credentials and were authorized to be seated and vote as regular delegates.

For the office of president of the convention the "radicals" nominated John Hall of Mason County, while the "conservatives" put forward as their candidate J. H. Brown of Kanawha County. The latter withdrew and Mr. Hall was chosen.

## "Endorsed by a Baker's Dozen"

E. R. Hall of Taylor County was nominated for secretary, his election being urged on the ground of his having been persecuted at home on account of his politics – It is evident from the discussion that quite a number of the delegates had been driven from their counties and needed financial assistance.

A Business Committee of nine was appointed, composed of Messrs. Van Winkle, Brown (of Kanawha), Hall (of Marion), Irvine, Sheets, Parker, Chapman, Caldwell, and Hagar. This became the "steering committee" of the convention.

The question of seating representatives who had not been elected then arose.

According to Mr. Stuart, seating them was the only way by which the counties not sending regularly accredited representatives could get a hearing. A slight irregularity was not worth noticing, he argued, to which Mr. Willey readily agreed, adding that "these are revolutionary times. The house is on fire and we cannot be very technical."

He said he would vote to admit them "on a venture," remembering, probably, his own irregular beginnings as a United States Senator.

The "representatives" were seated without further discussion.

Later in the convention, the delegate from Fayette County resigned and appointed his successor. In the discussion Mr. Pomeroy said: "Now, it is a singular thing, with a lot of Union soldiers in the county, a man comes here and claims to be a representative on this floor, endorsed by a single baker's dozen…"

Pomeroy's remarks were echoed by Delegate Bering, who stated, "Are we a regularly constituted deliberative body, regulated by law, or are we a mass meeting that any gentleman can come into and take a seat and draw pay from the treasury?"

## Defaulting on Debt Owed to Southerners

On the following day, eight standing committees were appointed – Fundamental and General Provisions; County Organization; Legislative Department; Executive Department; Judiciary; Taxation and Finance; Education; and Schedule. The convention transacted no more business this day, but adjourned to meet Friday, November 29, 1861.

By this time it had become apparent that the delegates were in real earnest in their attempt to make the new constitution more liberal than the one under which they had lived as Virginians. Such matters as popular education, universal white male suffrage, voting by ballot, and internal improvements were given much attention.

On November 30th Brown, of Kanawha, introduced the following resolution:

*"Resolved, That the state of Kanawha ought to assume a just and equitable proportion of the state debt of Virginia; and in doing so, to discriminate between its friends and foes, by first paying the bonds now held bona fide by her own loyal citizens; next, the bonds held bona fide by other loyal citizens of the United States not residents of the state of Kanawha; and the excess, if any, to the other bondholders, pro rata. Also, that it is unwise and impolitic to introduce the discussion of the slavery question into the deliberations of this convention."*

## Enlarging Kanawha's Borders

Monday, December 2, 1861, the Committee on Boundaries reported to the convention.

To the thirty-nine original counties that were to initially make up the new state, they added Pocahontas, Greenbrier, Monroe, Mercer, McDowell, Buchanan and Wise.

Additionally, Craig, Giles, Bland, Tazewell, Russell, Lee, Scott, Jefferson, Berkeley, Morgan, Hampshire, Hardy, Pendleton, Highland, Bath, Alleghany, Clark, Warren, Shenandoah, Page, Rockingham, Augusta, Rockbridge and Botetourt were to be given the opportunity of voting for annexation to the new state later in the coming year.

The report was taken up and discussed section by section.

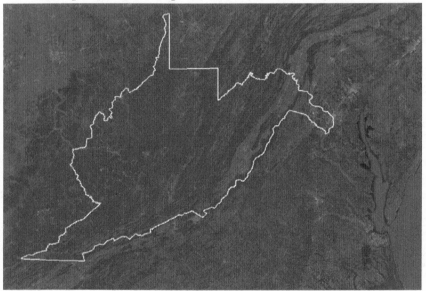

MAP: One of the many proposed borders for the new state.
*Image courtesy NOAA*

## Choosing a Name: Western Virginia or Kanawha

Mr. Sensel moved that "Kanawha" be stricken out, stating as his reason, that he was a Virginian and proud of the name.

Mr. Parker agreed and added that Kanawha would be confused with the county. A number of members testified to the unpopularity of the name with their constituents. Mass meetings had been held in many counties, protesting against it.

With these objections Mr. Lamb, of Ohio County, had little sympathy, although he had lived in Virginia for thirty years. "During that time what have we received here but oppression and outrage from the state of Virginia? What has been the policy of Virginia throughout? Are we going to keep that policy along with the name, when we came here for the very purpose of revolutionizing that policy in every respect almost in which it is possible for us to do so? No, gentlemen, no, I want to cut loose from these recollections. I have no hesitation in proclaiming to this convention and my constituents that there is nothing in the conduct of the state of Virginia to the people of Western Virginia that entitles her or the name to our attachment."

Mr. Caldwell remarked that Western Virginia had been a distinct name for years.

Mr. Willey said his people objected to "Kanawha" because it was hard to spell, while Mr. Lauck startled the other delegates by asserting that his constituents were not willing to have the new state at all if "Virginia" was stricken out. To this Mr. Van Winkle retorted that what he feared was that some of the gentlemen "intend to be Virginians after we have separated from Virginia. If we are so servile to old Virginia now that we are about casting off the fetters, if we cannot forget our servile habits, but must cringe and bow to old Virginia, I think. Sir, this movement had better stop precisely where it is now."

The speaker concluded by suggesting that there was a "suspiciously strong affection for the flesh-pots of Egypt."

Mr. Stuart replied to Mr. Van Winkle, displaying considerable warmth of feeling. His position was that Van Winkle and the others born outside the state of Virginia should not arrogate to themselves the responsibility of deciding the name of the new state.

"It is a familiar name. It is a name to speak, that of West Virginia."

Mr. Van Winkle was a native of the state of New York, and attorney for the Baltimore & Ohio Railroad.

It is evident that he was distrusted by the other members, for an undercurrent of hostility was apparent at all times when Mr. Van Winkle had the floor.

Mr. Willey was confident the new convention could adopt a new name if it saw fit, as it had already changed the previous ordinance so as to include some additional counties. His attitude toward "West Virginia" was dictated solely by the wishes of his constituents.

On the final vote the name "West Virginia" received thirty votes, "Kanawha" nine, "Western Virginia" two, "Alleghany" two, and "Augusta" one.

## Silencing the Voters of West Virginians

An argument now arose over the length of time a person should have to live in the state in order to qualify for voting. So liberal were the views of some of the members that Mr. Brown protested, alleging that the object seemed to be that of alluring voters from other states.

He opposed such liberality because he "wanted people to come here to live, not merely to vote."

His ideas did not prevail, however, and the length of residence was fixed at thirty days.

On Wednesday, December 4th, the important question of the electoral franchise was discussed. At the outset it was evident that there was a strong movement on foot to disqualify all but known Union men.

Said Mr. Caldwell, of Marshall County: "In my own county, in several counties that I think I could name, where the Secessionist element prevails, what will be the result in the formation of the new state? Why, Sir, where that element prevails, the Secessionists will override the Union party. They may go to the polls and elect officers, while the result will be that those persons so elected will refuse to qualify; and thus the organization in these counties will be defeated."

Mr. Willey stated that "the brave boys who are now standing up for these rights in the Union were of the poorer classes."

Mr. Hagar brought out the information that in his county the people had been ordered to join the Confederacy – and did so.

Mr. Parker declared roundly that men were "committing treason with as little compunction as they have in shooting squirrels."

Again Mr. Brown took the opposing view, by affirming that the proposed act would disfranchise a large number of Union men, and, "I dare say, many in this very house; for I have no doubt there are those in this house who have 'given aid and comfort to the rebellion' by furnishing provisions and shelter to their friends and relatives in the rebel army."

The following day the delegates debated the report of a committee which had advocated the viva voce method of voting. Mr.

Stuart said he had never seen any good result from voting by ballot and that how a man voted was known anyhow.

"I like this independent way of voting -- coming up and declaring how we vote. It seems to me it inculcates principles of independence."

He reminded his audience of the vote in May on secession, and asked if there would not have been a different showing if voting by ballot had prevailed.

Mr. Stuart's meaning is puzzling, in view of the fact that he was speaking in opposition to the secret ballot. If he had been arguing in its favor, we might assume he meant to suggest that the open method of voting prevented Union men from voting against secession, where the Secessionists predominated. The sole inference remaining is that if the secret ballot had been used, more votes in the western counties would have been cast for secession.

## West Virginia & "Rebel" Counties

It may be remarked in passing that all speakers from Secessionist counties told the same story, apparently with the idea of winning the goodwill of the other delegates. However, either the Union majority was a figment of their imagination or it was composed of a very pusillanimous set of men. Otherwise, the numerically weaker Secessionists would have been the ones intimidated.

The question was dropped for the present, while the convention proceeded to consider the inclusion of Wise and Buchanan counties. Mr. Brown thought it a good thing, because no one desired to have a "little picayune state."

They should adhere to "the good old American principle, which was to hold on to all the territory we get" and Mr. Stuart reminded the delegates that if these counties were cut off the state would lose one representative in Congress.

Mr. Pomeroy could not understand why they wanted to annex counties in which Secessionism ran rampant, to which Mr. Brown replied that "to cut off counties because they were for secession was a very dangerous game; and if you attempt to play it on principle I do not see where it would stop," a  plain admission that a great multitude of counties in the proposed new state were Southern in their sympathies, and, consequently, opposed to cutting loose from Virginia.

The motion to include the two counties was lost.

The same question arose over McDowell County. Mr. Walker, with no apparent intention of being humorous, remarked that he had been there in June, and "had found quite a number of men who were Union in their hearts although they dared not say so."

Always the frankest man on the floor was Mr. Hall, of Marion County, who boldly spoke for the inclusion of all border counties, in order to get a line with natural boundaries. It was of no great importance whether they wanted to come in or not. This convention was the sovereign people of West Virginia, and was bound by no previous act.

Mr. Carskadon stated that while only between sixty and seventy men had voted for representatives to the convention he felt sure that there were more Union men than that in what become known as "the Free State of McDowell."

Mr. Stevenson said, "If I could be satisfied that these counties of Mercer, Monroe, Greenbrier, and Pocahontas were made up of any considerable number of loyal people, I would favor it. But I have not been, and I am not, satisfied of the fact."

Mr. Parker, to ease Mr. Stevenson's conscience, remarked that the convention as a whole represented but a small faction of the state; and Mr. Brown adduced the further information that they were including counties that had given large majorities for secession. The Union men in these counties were being protected by a Union army, composed of men from other states.

In Logan, Boone and Wayne Counties a man who spoke in favor of the Union was taken to Richmond and tried for treason, said Mr. Brown. Yet thus far there had been no objection to including these counties.

Mr. Willey was of the opinion that the convention had no right to add more counties, to which Mr. Hall retorted that the convention could do anything "because the whole proceedings were irregular. It has not been very long since some gentlemen who are here could not have come here, and the time is even yet that some gentlemen within counties included here are not here; and we know very well the reason why the counties, in reference to which we are now proposing to take action, could not be represented here, are represented by very few votes, or by some means that is not exactly a vote at all."

The convention, at any rate, said Mr. Hall, represented the people more closely than the legislature did. "At the time a certain portion of the citizens of the state of Virginia were enabled to congregate themselves at the City of Wheeling and at a time when those in rebellion against the government held other parts, and being very impatient they went to work to form themselves into a new state including a few counties. Let me say a fact that is known, that this thing commenced at a time when some of the most prominent movers in the matter dared not go to their homes. As I before remarked, our necessity requires that if they are not with us in sentiment, in all events their territory must be with us."

Mr. Brown hereupon stated that before the people of the border counties could vote it would be necessary to station a Union Army there.

The discussion as to the wisdom of absorbing Secessionist counties continued the following day. The large-state advocates were now in the saddle, and rode triumphantly through the opposition, who desired a small, compact state, composed of counties where there was at least a considerable Union minority.

Said Mr. Willey: "The county of Calhoun spurns our invitation, it is said. The county of Nicholas spurns our invitation. That is her own fault, sir. She might have been represented here; and if she sees proper to stay at home and allow us to fix it for her, she has no right to complain."

An interesting sidelight is turned on the events of the preceding months by the remarks of Mr. Hagar: "I am informed by the delegate from Wayne, notwithstanding Ziegler had a regiment there, that all the elections had to be guarded by his regiment. I do not know how many elections were held in Cabell County. However, they held one somewhere, and the county is represented. Boone, which has eight places of holding elections, by a detachment being sent from Kanawha held an election at two precincts. The returns are not here; the man I sent may have been captured. If it required a military force to hold an election, if Cabell County, which borders on the Ohio River, had to have a military force to hold an election there; if Boone had to have a military force to hold an election at two points; if a detachment went up and held an election there, and got into a comer

157

of Raleigh and held an election there, with what difficulty are the counties represented!"

The speaker closed by saying that he knew personally the people of those counties were opposed to the new state.

Mr. Soper confirmed this, and added that the earlier conventions were all irregular bodies; that the members of the so-called legislature were not legally chosen, and that they violated their instructions when they provided for the formation of a new state instead of merely reconstructing the old state. The people, thus far, had never indicated that they wished to separate from old Virginia. Mr. Soper seemed to think that although most of the counties included in the boundaries of the proposed new state were full of Secessionists, these persons would finally become reconciled to the new state – certainly, if the South lost.

Mr. Soper was referred to by the chairman as "the gentleman from New York now representing Tyler County."

Mr. Van Winkle stated that he doubted "if there were any counties this side of the Alleghenies where there were nothing but Secessionists."

The North had been led to believe that there were nothing but Unionists this side of the Alleghenies. Mr. Van Winkle here admits that the Unionists were few in number.

Mr. Simmons, of Randolph County, was positive that there were some Union men in his county, and also in Pendleton and Hardy. An election had been held, he stated, in one corner of Tucker County, by a Union company, and a member had been chosen to the state legislature.

Mr. Carskadon frankly admitted that "at the precinct at which I was elected – they did not know at the time I was a candidate – there were but thirty-nine votes cast."

Mr. Lamb, of Ohio County, whose Unionism could not be doubted, declared that out of two thousand voters in Hampshire County, only one hundred and ninety-five votes had been cast and he had heard that of these, one hundred were cast by soldiers. Mr. Carskadon confirmed this and added that only thirty-nine were the votes of citizens of the state.

So frank were the admissions of the southern loyalty of the people of Western Virginia that the convention felt it necessary to reject a motion to have the debates published.

January 7, 1862, a petition from Calhoun County was read as follows:

*"The humble memorial of the undersigned qualified voters in and for the County of Calhoun, respectfully represent that they were unable to hold an election for a delegate to your convention, as they desired to do and would have done, but for the following reasons: There is no sheriff, clerk or justices in our county, and no court has been held in said county since June last; all the county officers are or have been engaged in the rebellion, so that there was no one to hold an election. The undersigned compose nearly the whole loyal voters in the said county, for, in fact, at the election upon the ordinance of secession, there were but fifty votes cast in said county against it."*

The petition was unanimously granted, Mr. Van Winkle remarking that it would not do to hold too strictly to the law.

## Logan County's "Representative" in Convention

In January 1862, the Northern politicians assembled in Wheeling voted to seat a delegate to the convention purportedly representing the people of Logan County.

Though Logan County's elected state legislator was loyally serving the county in the Richmond legislature, a man arrived in Wheeling with a petition of fifteen signatures – most of which were relation – claiming to be the elected representative of the people of Logan County.

Without any debate, the convention seated the man. It was later learned that the individual did not even live in Logan County, however, still yet, this revelation had no bearing on his standing in the convention.

After this there could be no pretense of legality.

When questioned about why he was representing a county he did not even live within, the man replied, "there was to be found no one who was willing to run the risk of representing Logan County."

# Disenfranchising West Virginia's Southern Counties

Established in 1867, West Virginia University, the State of West Virginia's first public university was established just a handful of miles from the Pennsylvania-line – more than 250 miles from McDowell County.

The workers of northern West Virginia enjoyed the right to unionize early in the 20th century, while the miners in the southern portion of the state had to rise up in a bloody civil war a decade following World War I, simply to have this most basic human right – fighting their own state government and its overtly corrupt governor and state police force which had chosen the side of northern capitalists over the workers of their own state.

Even today, a century and a half following the disruption of Virginia, there exists a clear and undeniable disenfranchisement between southern West Virginia and northern West Virginia.

According to August 2015 Department of Labor statistics, in the southern portion of the state, Mingo County's unemployment rate was 14.6%, Logan County 12.6%, Wyoming County 11.2% and McDowell County 14.2% -- the highest of any region in the state. These numbers are in stark contrast to the state's northern counties: Monongalia County registered an unemployment rate of 6.0%, Doddridge County 5.9% and Berkeley County registering 5.6%.

The list of hardships the people in Mingo, McDowell, Mercer and roughly a dozen other southern West Virginia counties presently face can all be traced back to a single event which occurred on January 13, 1862:

On this date, Harmon Sinsel, a delegate from Taylor County to the Constitutional Convention made some extremely illuminating admissions while the subject of the apportionment of representatives was under discussion. He referred to the border counties as "deadly Secessionist in sentiment and feeling," and predicted that after the rebellion only Secessionists would be elected to public office.

"Who denies that McDowell, Wyoming, Raleigh, Calhoun, Gilmer, Braxton, Clay, Tucker, Randolph, Webster, Nicholas, Boone, Logan, Pocahontas, Roane, Wirt, Monroe, and Greenbrier – add to that Barbour and many others – are all dominated by the spirit of the rebellion?"

It is interesting to observe that the manuscript record of the debate contains no answer or denial of this very serious allegation.

Had his allegations not been true, had there been the slightest doubt of the sentiment of the people of these and other unnamed counties, Mr. Sinsel would have discovered that he had disturbed a hornet's nest. The strong Union men in the convention would have accepted the challenge, had there been any facts upon which to base their counter-argument.

Any discerning person can recognize that the delegates present in Wheeling took Mr. Sinsel's charges seriously and understood all too well the truth in what he was saying – immediately following his speech, the discussion of the convention narrowed down to one specific question: How could the apportionment of representatives in the legislature be arranged so as to give the larger Secessionist counties of the southern region of the state as little power as possible?

We can trace many of the problems presently affecting Southern West Virginia: incredibly high unemployment, lack of educational opportunities, generational welfare dependence, etc., to the effort of the convention to silence the influence and general welfare of the proposed new state's southern residents.

For had the northern leadership placed the state's first public university in a more centralized location, education would have been far more accessible for the common citizens of what is presently underprivileged areas – providing the laborers of the early 20th century alternatives to working as slaves in dangerous coal mines of the 1920s – a move that would forever change the direction of the southern and eastern counties.

Southern West Virginia, it seems, has never been seen by representatives of Wheeling or Morgantown as anything more than a distant foreign colony, a remote outpost blessed with a rich abundance of natural resources – the treasure of which has always been carried far away without any concern or commitment from the distant industrialists to reinvest into the local communities and people who supplied their fortunes.

After a century of mining, all that southern West Virginia has to show for it are empty holes and in impoverished people – all of which has occurred with, at best, the blessing of the northern controlled state government, and at worst, its invitation.

161

# The Slavery Question

The slavery question, as was anticipated, aroused heated discussion among the delegates serving in Wheeling.

Gordon Battelle, a Methodist minister and a native of Ohio, introduced a series of resolutions providing, first, that no slaves should come into the state for permanent residence after the adoption of the constitution; second, that the legislature should provide for the mitigation of the evils of slavery until July 4, 1862, when the institution should be abolished.

Battelle later modified his first proposition so that all children born of slave parents after July 4, 1865, should be free, and that the people of the state, when they voted on the constitution, should also vote on the question of gradual emancipation.

There was, however, plenty of feeling in the convention against the abolition of slavery in any form, and the body declined to go on record as favoring such legislation. They did incorporate into the constitution a clause whereby both slaves and free African-Americans should not be permitted to enter the state.

# The First Constitution of West Virginia

The first draft of the first constitution of West Virginia resembled very much the organic law of the old state, but there are some notable points of divergence.

Voting by ballot took the place of voice voting, which was authorized to continue under the Virginia Constitution of 1851. Also, the registration of voters was provided for, and the legislature was instructed to establish a system of public schools.

The fourth Thursday in April 1862, was designated as the day upon which the constitution was to be submitted to the voters of the state, and commissioners were appointed to make the necessary arrangements. In the event of the ratification of the constitution, the returns were to be reported to the legislature and its consent obtained to the separation.

This done, Congress was to be asked to admit the new state.

When the new constitution was finally submitted to the voters, it was adopted by the suspiciously large majority of 20,622 to 440.

*Residents of Northern States Permitted to Vote:*

The soldiers' vote was announced as 7,579 to 131.

In order to make the result more imposing, commissioners were sent out to the various camps so that the soldiers would be permitted to vote.

In this manner, citizens of Pennsylvania, Ohio and Indiana were enabled to vote, so long as they verbally stated that they had been in the state for at least thirty-days.

The vote in some of the counties was reported as follows: Ohio, 1,805 to 8 ; Marshall, 1,433 to 56 ; Hancock, 373 to 5 ; Hardy, 76 to ; Morgan, 362 to ; Pendleton, 181 to ; Pleasants, 253 to 0; Randolph, 167 to 13; Roane, 159 to 0; Tucker, 45 to 1 ; Wayne, 85 to 2 ; Marion, 965 to 3 ; Lewis, 596 to 4; Wood, 1,222 to 1 ; Harrison, 1,074 to 7; Monongalia, 1,415 to 128; Taylor, 716 to 5; Barbour, 471 to 0; Brooke, 448 to 1; Cabell, 106 to 0; Gilmer, 383 to 1 ; Hampshire, 75 to 9.

*Six Counties Overpower More Than Twenty:*

No returns were ever received from Calhoun, Greenbrier, Logan, McDowell, Mercer, Monroe, Preston, Raleigh and Wyoming counties.

The four Northern Panhandle counties furnished more than one—third of the entire civilian vote for the new constitution. The Eastern Panhandle cast a total of five hundred and thirty votes. Along the border of Virginia only one county, Hardy, reported that a poll had even been taken. The measure was practically adopted by a vote of six counties against the silent protests of more than twenty other localities.

It is a poor argument to say that many of these counties were in possession of the Confederates at the time of the election, for this is equivalent to saying that they were controlled by a majority of their own citizens. Yet if four hundred and seventy—one persons in Barbour County were permitted to vote, why were not the other qualified voters permitted to do the same?

Why did the poll show the curious anomaly of a practically unanimous vote in the strongest Secessionist counties? All these questions and others present themselves for serious consideration, and the more they are studied the more convinced must one become that the present state of West Virginia is comprised mainly of counties that were opposed to severing from the old state.

A letter to the *Wheeling Intelligencer*, on April 30, 1862, from Braxton County reads:

*"The election was a mere farce, a thing done in the corner by those who feared the light and wished to possess themselves of power not for the sake of being useful to their country and fellow-citizens but for selfish ends alone. . . . Not more than one hundred votes were polled in a county of some 1,100 voters and our legislature was elected by a still smaller number of votes."*

The *Intelligencer*, the same day, printed a letter from a Colonel in the Union army stationed in one of the interior counties, to the effect that he had been instructed to prevent people from voting against the new-state constitution.

A letter to the *Wheeling Press*, Nov. 27, 1862, declared that the last time there had been a free election in West Virginia was when delegates had been elected to the Richmond Convention.

Not one-fifth of the normal vote of the county had been cast at any election. The writer asserts that it was dangerous to vote against any measure in which the new state was interested.

*"Could there be a fair expression of the people within the bounds of the new state, I do not doubt that the vote would be overwhelmingly against it."*

### An Ancient Problem Continues

Regrettably, voter suppression and tales of dishonest elections have marred the history of West Virginia, specifically that of the state's southernmost counties, for well over a century.

The course of crushing the will of the voters in West Virginia's southern wilderness during the American Civil War set a precedence that would continue on for generations.

In 1910, Rankin Wiley, a West Virginia Democrat, challenged the Congressional seat of James A. Hughes, a Canadian carpet-bagger who had served in the Kentucky legislature before moving to the Mountain State where he served in the West Virginia Senate and received an appointment as postmaster of Huntington. The Canadian-born politician was elected to the United States House of Representatives in 1900, representing the Fifth Congressional District of West Virginia.

Allegations of voter fraud ran rampant during the contest, especially in the counties of Mingo and McDowell.

Ultimately, fraud was admitted to in at least nine precincts in Mingo County and in "The Free State of McDowell," the Republican president of the county court refused to appoint Democratic challengers although the law of West Virginia clearly stated that it was his duty to make such appointment on the nomination of the Democratic chairman.

According to congressional records, when "Democratic challengers attempted to serve they were either arrested or driven from the polls."[44]

Things were so lawless in McDowell County that, according to Wiley's testimony, he "had been warned not to go into the county to make speeches for fear of personal violence…"

In the end, the results of the entire election were discarded and the Canadian-American was allowed to maintain his Congressional seat, representing the counties of McDowell and Mingo.

Additional schisms plagued this region of the state for decades to come – In 1933, *The Charleston Daily Mail*[45] reported on allegations of widespread election fraud in McDowell County in the November 1932 election.

According to the *Beckley Post—Herald*[46], in 1946 elections, fraud was charged in ten counties of southern West Virginia and "enough evidence was offered to persuade a subcommittee of the United States senate to send out a trained crew of investigators to trace down the fraud and report back to the Senate."

Even today, the voters of Southern West Virginia can hardly go to the polls and be confident that their voice will be heard.

There is an old anecdote that tells of a Mingo County politician who was strolling through a family cemetery when he suddenly

---

[44] *Congressional Edition*, Volume 7240, p.59

[45] *The Charleston Daily Mail*, 9 Feb. 1933, "House Election Report Adopted"

[46] *The Beckley Post -- Herald*, 8 Feb. 1949, "A Case for the F.B.I."

stopped and stated, "You know, I'm a strong believer in equal voting rights... I believe the folks buried in the far back of this cemetery have just as much right to vote as those buried in the front."

"Vote early and vote often" has long been the joke in Southern West Virginia on election day; unfortunately, a 2015 report published by the Alexandria, Virginia, based Public Interest Legal Foundation (PILF) revealed that the ancient problems that plagued West Virginia a century ago remain to this day.

The foundation alleged that three West Virginia counties actually have more registered voters than people of voting age that are alive in the county[47].

In a published statement, the foundation confirmed that election officials in the West Virginia counties of Mingo, Lincoln and McDowell were sent statutory notice letters informing them of the discrepancies.

According to the foundation, Mingo County's registration rate was 108% of the number of voting age citizens, alive, in the county, while Lincoln County's registration rate was 107% and McDowell County had 103% of their living citizens alive.

"Having more registrants than eligible citizens alive indicates that election officials have failed to properly maintain voter rolls," stated the release.

"Corrupted voter rolls provide the perfect environment for voter fraud," said J. Christian Adams, President and General Counsel of PILF.

I have often heard people compare the government of West Virginia to a totalitarian state, which gives the following quote made by Joseph Stalin, General secretary of the Central Committee of the Communist Party of the Soviet Union (1922-1952), even more credence:

*"It is enough that the people know there was an election. The people who cast the votes decide nothing. The people who count the votes decide everything."*

---

[47] "Scores of Counties Put on Notice About Corrupted Voter Rolls" Public Interest Legal Foundation, August 27, 2015.

From a young child, I learned real quickly of the importance the citizenry of Southern West Virginia place upon politics.

When I was about ten-years-old, I remember watching my uncle staple the campaign sign of whichever candidate he was supporting to a telephone pole, only to return that afternoon to discover the opposing candidate's sign had been stapled over his. My uncle's response—reach into his trunk and pull out yet another sign and nail it over the other two. Never would you remove an opponent's sign… that would be considered dishonorable!

I'm not sure why these politicians had such a hold over the local people in those "hollers," but whatever it was, the people took politics serious – many a man lost his life over words spoken about a politician in Southern West Virginia.

Sadly, even with such a fierce loyalty to their elected officials for over a century, here we stand in the contemporary world of the twenty-first century and our beloved state is at the bottom of the list on all the good things and at the top on all of the bad things – we can't even say, "Thank God for Mississippi" anymore.

West Virginia serves as the only state in the Union where less than half of the civilian population works[48] and a recent survey revealed that 28.1 percent of its population admits to altering "their mood with drugs almost every day;"[49] it is clear that the State of West Virginia is on the brink of total ruin.

But why? Why is West Virginia in such a state of disarray? What is the course of events that has led to the present-day situation we find in places such as Mingo and McDowell counties, where the unemployment rate is near 15 percent?

There is no one answer to this very deep question, however, one would be remiss if he did not cast a large portion of this blame at the feet of the politicians who have continued this deviant game of making merchandise of the people.

Another culprit is we as the voters. We have allowed ourselves to be caught up into the rhetoric preached by both wings of the same bird. We have ceased to hold our politicians accountable because of

---

[48] MarketWatch.com, Steve Goldstein. "The only state where less than half of all civilians work" March 19, 2015.

[49] WashingtonPost.com, Christopher Ingraham. "West Virginia is the capital of mind-altering drug use" April 1, 2015.

the D or R beside their name and we have ceased to consider new ideas for this very same reason.

Our state is on the brink of total collapse, these are indeed perilous times and we as citizens must not look to the leaders of parties for direction, we must direct them.

We must see things for what they are and demand more. We must consider new ideas and recognize that the issues of the early-1920s are obsolete; hence our laws must be changed in order to attract new business. We must understand that one man is not the creator of all our problems and neither will one man be the solution to all of our problems.

These are hard truths, but it's time we get honest with ourselves before we lose everything.


## The "Legislature of Virginia" Authorizes West Virginia

An extra session of "the Virginia legislature" was called for May 5, 1865, and on that day thirty-one delegates and ten Senators came together in Wheeling, for the purpose of carrying out that section of the United States Constitution which says that no new state shall be formed out of an existing state without the consent of the latter. These forty-one men were held to be capable of acting for a million free citizens of Virginia.

Horace Greeley in his "American Conflict" makes a typical defense of the action of the legislature in assenting to the division of Virginia. He says, "This action was taken throughout on the assumption that the loyal people of a state constitute the state; that traitors and rebels who repudiate all respect for and loyalty to the constitution and government of the country have no right to control that government and that those people of any state who heartily recognize and faithfully discharge their obligations . . . have a right to full and perfect protection from the Republic."[50]

In his address to the assembly, Governor Pierpont attacked the position of those who pronounced the whole affair to be a revolutionary proceeding; however, in his attempt to show that all constitutional and legal forms had been and would in the future be

---

[50] Greeley, Horace. *A History of the Great Rebellion in the United States of America, 1860-'64.* (1866) p. 519.

complied with, he found himself navigating a maze of twisted thoughts and illogical reasoning.

Answering the charge that the new state would be established on an act of revolution, he said: "Those who urge this objection do not understand the history, geography, and social relations of the state."

The reader may well ask what these things had to do with an abstract question of political theory. However, the situation did not call for close reasoning and clear thinking, for the mock legislature had made up its mind long before. After going through the formality of appointing a committee to consider the question, it gave its consent to the formation of a new state in the name of and as the representatives of the sovereign people of Virginia.

### The act reads:

*"Be it enacted by the General Assembly, That the consent of the legislature of Virginia be and the same is hereby given to the formation and erection of the state of West Virginia within the jurisdiction of this state to include the counties of, according to the boundaries and under the provisions set forth in the constitution for the said state of West Virginia and the schedule thereto annexed, proposed by the convention which assembled at Wheeling on the 26th day of November, 1861.*

*"Second, Be it further enacted. That the consent of the legislature be and the same is hereby given that the counties of Berkeley, Jefferson, and Frederick shall be included in and form part of the state of West Virginia, whenever the voters of said counties shall ratify and assent to the said constitution at an election held for the purpose at such time and under such regulations as the commissioners named in the said schedule may prescribe.*

*"Third, Be it further enacted, That this act shall be transmitted by the Executive to the Senators and Representatives of this Commonwealth in Congress, together with a certified original of the said constitution and schedule, and the said Senators and Representatives are hereby requested to use their endeavors to obtain*

the consent of Congress to the admission of the state of West Virginia into the Union.

"Fourth, This act shall be enforced from and after its passage."

Chapter
Eleven

# West Virginia
# Goes to Congress

The Restored Government of Virginia's relationship with the United States Congress was rocky at best – on one hand, the Restored Government proved loyal to the Lincoln Administration and the Federal Union when the Government needed a buffer against Dixie.

On the other hand, the pure brazenness and unconstitutionality of the Restored Government presented a moral dilemma that even the most adherent Union men struggled to reckon with.

In the early part of 1862, the United States Congress faced a minor constitutional crises when the lower house of the Federal legislature refused to seat two men claiming to have been elected to the House of Representatives from Virginia.

171

The two men, Charles H. Upton and Joseph Segar, were loyalists whose election to the House caused great concern for members of Congress.

## Joseph Segar: Elected to Congress on 25 Votes

A native of King William County, a locality on the eastern shore peninsula, Joseph Segar arrived in Washington after an October 1861 special election called for by Francis Pierpont, the Wheeling-appointed acting governor of Virginia.

Located deep in the heart of Virginia's plantation country, King William County was as staunchly southern as any locality one would find in the heart of the Deep South – The county was so southern in its loyalties that in May 1861, voters in the community chose secession from the Union by a margin of 496 to 0.

Despite the overwhelming mentality of locals siding in favor of the Cotton Republic, Governor Pierpont appointed the fourth Tuesday in October 1861 to serve as the day when special elections should be held across the Commonwealth for the purpose of filling the vacancies that existed in the Virginia delegation to Congress.

It was admitted that the Secessionists controlled all but the two Congressional districts of Virginia, but according to the prevailing theory the loyal citizens, no matter how small their number, might constitute the electorate.

In Segar's case, only 25 individuals from his entire Congressional district cast a vote in the election and all were made in his favor.

The poll had been taken at Hampton, Virginia, and was certified by the clerk and two freeholders.

Pierpont thereupon signed the certificate of election and dispatched Segar to Congress, authorizing him to represent tens of thousands of individuals who claimed to be citizens of the Confederate States of America – with only twenty-five votes to his name.

Once in Congress, the Election Committee expressed the opinion that the Wheeling convention had exceeded its power in continuing to act as a legislative body for Virginia.

On February 10, 1862, the committee released its findings:

*According to the committee's report, the act of the convention providing for a special election was a usurpation of the duties of the legislature. Even assuming that up to this point the proceedings were regular, what followed was clearly irregular. Instead of calling upon the sheriffs to conduct the election as prescribed by law, the Governor in his proclamation "entreated the loyal voters to hold an election."*

Mr. Segar admitted that there was no poll taken anywhere but at Hampton, and frankly confessed that he would not have known of the Governor's proclamation had it not been that a certain man, stopping over in Hampton, had read it in the *National Intelligencer.* He informed Mr. Segar of the fact and the latter decided to become a candidate. The committee held that under the circumstances the contestant could have no claim to a seat in the House.

*Joseph Segar's Defense:*
Segar's defense of his claim deserves to rank as a great piece of congressional humor. The issue, he said, was not whether he should be seated; that was of no importance whatsoever. The real question involved the right of a loyal citizen to sit in the House of Representatives. It was true that some of the petty forms were not complied with, but they were swept away by the old maxim de minimis non curat lex – a common law principle whereby judges will not sit in judgment of extremely minor transgressions of the law.

The Wheeling Convention, in his opinion, could do anything the sovereign people could do, but even if it could not, the situation would not be altered, for Governor Pierpont had signed his election certificate, and all people knew that Pierpont was the lawful Governor of Virginia.

As for the smallness of the vote cast, the House could not take this into consideration while it had officially recognized the Wheeling government which had been set up by a very small minority of the people.

William Dawes, of Massachusetts, effectually disposed of any further arguments the petitioner might have presented by stating that the only pertinent question was the legality of the election.

The convention organized the "restored legislature" and put it under the constitution and laws of Virginia; then it proceeded to act as though no legislature existed. In the case at hand, twenty-five men living near a hotel kept by the claimant cast their votes without form of law. "It is a mockery to representation itself," exclaimed the

Massachusetts lawmaker, adding, "It is a mockery to the freedom of election."

The committee's report was adopted and Mr. Segar was refused a seat in the House.

### Charles H. Upton: Elected to Congress Without an Election

Upton's case was reported from the committee Jan. 30, 1862, with adverse recommendation. The contestant had presented his credentials at the opening of the special session in July, as representative of the seventh district of Virginia. No objection had been raised until December 9, 1861, when a Mr. S. F. Beach appeared, contesting Mr. Upton's right to the seat.

February 26th the House took up the consideration of the committee's report. Beach, in his petition, alleged that on May 23rd not a single poll had been opened, owing partly to the presence of a large military force. Thus Upton could not have been legally elected, even though he had been a citizen of Virginia which, the petitioner said, he was not.

Upon the 24th of October an election was held in accordance with Pierpont's proclamation and a small vote was cast, all for the petitioner.

Upton should be unseated -- first, because no regular election had been conducted on May 23rd, and second, because Upton was a citizen of Ohio and could not represent the state of Virginia.

Ohio Republican, Samuel T. Worcester brushed aside the second objection and declared that the real question was one of fact, not whether a legal election could have taken place at the time, but whether it was physically possible under the circumstances.

No one doubted that the act annulling the election laws was a usurpation but it was effective at any rate. There was no evidence to show that any attempt had been made to comply with the laws of Virginia prescribing the mode of conducting elections in the present case. The contestant brought no certificate from the Governor or from any election board. He had not shown that a single legal vote had been cast for him, although there were documents exhibiting the fact that Mr. Beach had declared his candidacy and that ninety-five persons had cast their votes for him. These documents were not attested to in legal form.

Mr. Upton, however, rested his claim upon a poll of ten votes taken in Ball's Cross Road, Alexandria County, and certified to by a justice of the peace. "This was of no more value," said Congressman Worcester, "than the other alleged poll."

The committee had unanimously agreed that Upton was not entitled to a seat in the House.

Although some of the Representatives, fearing for their own seats, opposed the committee's report, Congressman Dawes bore down their objections by stating that Upton had come there "without the certificate of the Governor, without a certificate of an election board, and without the certificate of any man touching his right to his seat. He came here and induced the Clerk of the House to put his name upon the list of members.

"He was sworn in without so much as a vote of the House upon the question."

The last word for the defense was the reply of Mr. Sedgwick, who brought out the fact that none of the Virginia Representatives then in Congress had been elected according to the laws of the state.

They had been admitted on the ground that full compliance was impossible, and that at such a time technicalities should be passed over. The chief point of difference between the case of the Representatives from Western Virginia and that of Mr. Upton was that the latter had received fewer votes. But no law could be found anywhere prescribing the minimum number of votes a candidate must receive. To this the Massachusetts's politician retorted that the essential thing was not the number of votes but how they had been cast.

The crux of the whole situation was that no legal election had taken place or could take place under existing circumstances. In this opinion the House concurred and the action of the committee unseating Mr. Upton was sustained.

### Other Virginia Candidates to Congress

Two similar contests took place in the third session of the Thirty-seventh Congress of the United States (March 4, 1861- March 4, 1863) when J. B. McCloud and W. W. Wing appeared, each claiming to have been elected to serve as the 2nd Congressional District of Virginia's representative.

The election was conducted under the authority of three proclamations, one by General Dix commanding the department of Virginia, another by General Vielie who had permitted all males over twenty-one years of age to vote, regardless of residence.

Both McCloud and Wing, together with a Mr. McKenzie claiming a seat as representative from the Seventh Congressional District of Virginia, were refused seats in the House.

The schism revealed the level of lawlessness in Virginia and pointed to the fact that the Restored Government of Virginia was nothing more than one of several regional powers competing for control over the Commonwealth of Virginia during a time of great national peril and anarchy.

# Congress is Notified of "West Virginia"

May 29, 1862, Congress received its first official intimation that West Virginia would apply for admission into the Union. On that day Senator Willey brought the matter to the attention of the Senate by presenting a memorial from the so-called legislature of Virginia, asking that its consent be given to the formation of a new state within the boundaries of Virginia.

The U.S. Senate not only gave its consent to the division of the state, but urged the Senators and Representatives from Virginia to make every effort to overcome the opposition in the House of Representatives.

Never before in our history has the country witnessed the spectacle of a state legislature petitioning Congress to agree to the cutting up of the dominion for which it was supposed to make laws.

Another memorial was presented, purported to have come from the people of West Virginia. It recited the wrongs that West Virginia had endured for forty years; enlarged on the good effect which the admission of West Virginia would have on the country as a whole; and declared finally that some "wolves in sheep's clothing" had gotten into the convention and prevented the passage of a free-state constitution.

This was unfortunate, but unless Congress admitted West Virginia at once there was grave danger that by the time the legislature reassembled there would be sufficient representation from the eastern counties and the Valley to rescind the former action consenting to division.

As for the constitutional objections, Virginia's Richmond Governor, John Letcher, and the disloyal members of the assembly had abdicated and the reorganizers had exercised their rights as the sovereign people to form a government, they noted.

Speaking from the floor of the United States Senate, Waitman T. Willey attempted to make heroes out of the delegates of the Wheeling Convention, boldly misrepresenting the facts, he entered into an explanation of the actions of the restored government, quoting Governor Pierpont to the effect that they had made only one change in the state constitution -- Willey did not think it necessary to explain that this one change which had been so blithely made was that of reducing the number of members in the General Assembly necessary to constitute a quorum. This was the only change needed in order to give a show of legality to the actions of the legislature. If the constitution could be changed in this one particular, it could be just as easily altered in any way the Wheeling government saw fit..

The Senate was told that the government organized by the June convention was for the whole state of Virginia and as such was recognized by the Federal authorities.

In August an adjourned session of the convention passed an ordinance, providing for the formation of a new state and the submission of the question to the voters. The latter had given their consent almost unanimously; the legislature was persuaded to agree to the division of the state; the constitution had been drawn up, and the question was now before Congress.

Mr. Willey gave an exhaustive list of reasons why the two sections of Virginia could never live in harmony, but when he declared that the passage of the West Virginia bill through Congress would "send a thrill of joy through 500,000 hearts" he was making a statement which he knew to be absolutely false.

Upon request of Senator Charles Sumner of Massachusetts, the question of the admission of West Virginia was referred to the Territorial Committee, of which Senator Benjamin Wade of Ohio was chairman.

On June 23rd the bill was reported and advanced to a second reading.

Three days later it was read a second time and taken up in Committee of the Whole.

An analysis of the Senate bill shows that someone had taken advantage of the committee's unfamiliarity with the situation in West Virginia, for not only were the forty-eight counties included, as had been provided for in the original act of the legislature, but there were added the counties of Berkeley, Jefferson, Clark, Warren, Frederick, Page, Shenandoah, Rockingham, Augusta, Highland, Bath, Rockbridge, Botetourt, Craig, and Alleghany.

## West Virginia: The Last Slave State Admitted into the Union

Senator Charles Sumner of Massachusetts, after the bill had been read, at once served notice that he would fight the measure so long as it did not contain a clause abolishing slavery at some time in the near future.

He then made a motion to insert a clause by which slavery was to be abolished altogether after July 4, 1863.

Senator John P. Hale of New Hampshire remarked that it would be a singular thing if the Senate, after admitting many states whose constitutions made slavery perpetual, should decline to admit the first state which had provided for the ultimate extinction of slavery.

Senator Willey declared that the Senator from Massachusetts was not familiar with the situation in West Virginia.

The 8,000 slaves in West Virginia, he asserted, were mainly house servants, who would be the very ones to suffer by immediate emancipation.

Benjamin Wade of Ohio admitted that the bill was open to much criticism, but averred that it had not been approved by the committee; it would serve their purpose of bringing up something which could be used as the basis of discussion. He objected to the emancipation clause as it stood, because it would make free a person born one day after July 4, 1863, and make slave one born the day before. A graduated system of emancipation was, in his opinion, far better.

The present bill should not be passed, but the Senate would do wrong in imposing severe and unprecedented conditions upon the proposed new state.

Further consideration was postponed until July 7th, when Willey attempted to have the Senate defer all prior orders and take up the bill. He declared that the state stood "with her heart bleeding; with all her industrial and commercial interests prostrate,"[51] and that unless some relief were given the Union men must take their families and find homes in the west.

The Senate refused to believe that West Virginia was bleeding to death, and Senator Willey's appeal went unheeded.

On July 14th Mr. Wade persuaded his colleagues to take up the West Virginia bill again.

Recurring to Mr. Sumner's amendment, the yeas and nays were ordered, with the result that the amendment was rejected by a vote of eleven to twenty-four.

The debate now centered around Mr. Wade's proposal that not only should slave children born after July 4, 1863, be free, but that all slaves under twenty-one at the time aforesaid should be free when they reached twenty-one years of age.

Mr. Willey urged with some show of reason that the chief effect of such a clause would be the transference of all slaves under twenty-one to the far south.

Slaveholders would not stand idly by and permit what they, in their warped mind, believed was their property to be taken away by process of law when they could prevent it.

Moreover, the secessionists in the state would use the abolition clause as a means to prevent the ratification of the constitution, which could only mean that the new state would never be formed.


## The Defection of Senator Carlile

Carlile gave unmistakable evidence of his opposition to the proposed bill by proposing an amendment, whereby the ordinance to be effective must be ratified by a vote of the majority of the voters of West Virginia.

Mr. Willey at once attacked the suggestion as one calculated to destroy all hope of forming a new state, since under the circumstances it would be impossible to get out anything like a full vote.

---

[51] U. S. Senate Debate on West Virginia Statehood. July 7, 1862. Extracted from the *Congressional Globe*.

Carlile answered that all he desired was the assurance that the people of West Virginia really did wish to break away from the old state. So far, he admitted, there had been no vote to indicate that such was their preference.

A majority of the voting population within the boundaries of West Virginia had never assented directly to any proposition put up to them so far.

The erection of imaginary lines between the sections of Virginia would serve no purpose in itself.

Replying to Joseph Pomeroy, who remarked that Carlile's evident purpose was to put off the measure until another session, adding that if the people of West Virginia did not send Senators favorable to it they could not expect to have the bill passed, Carlile returned that they would lose no time, since the new state could not be admitted before the following January and Congress would meet in December.

If by that time the people of West Virginia had drawn up a new constitution more in accord with the ideas of the Senate, why could not the measure be acted upon and the state admitted? No time need be lost.

In a moment of candor, Carlile informed his colleagues that eleven of the counties west of the Alleghenies had never been represented in any of the Wheeling conventions or in the reorganized legislature.

Three other counties had sent but one man; so it could truly be said that at least one third of the proposed new state had expressed no desire to leave Virginia.

When asked if the convention did not represent the whole people of West Virginia, Carlile replied that, while the chaotic condition of some of the counties has something to do with the light vote cast, even in the counties free from rebel troops little interest had been taken in any of the elections.

Mr. Wade expressed his surprise that these things were not brought out by Carlile in committee.

For the first time the Senate was being told that the Wheeling Convention did not represent the people of West Virginia.

## Keeping Slavery Legal

As the slavery question continued, Mr. Willey now offered as an amendment to the House bill (calling for the gradual emancipation of slaves) providing that no slaves should be brought into the state for permanent residence.

Mr. Lane moved an amendment to the amendment that all slaves under ten years of age on the 4th day of July, 1863, should be free on reaching the age of twenty-one years, and all between the ages of ten and twenty-one should be free when they became twenty-five years old.

Both amendments were accepted.

Senator Trumbull, who had consistently opposed the whole proposition, now recapitulated the case of the opposition. The general government had need of the present organization calling itself the government of Virginia, which state, if it was further reclaimed, would need the provisional government of Wheeling.

Again, there was no getting away from the fact that a state was being admitted in which slavery would exist for several generations.

The formation of a new state would be of no assistance to the loyal citizens of West Virginia, since their arms could not thereby be made more effective against the rebels.

Internal war would not cease necessarily after the admission of West Virginia to statehood. "When this war shall have subsided and we shall have a settlement of the controversies which are now pending, who can tell the embarrassments that will arise out of our having divided Virginia at this time? It will be too late then to put Virginia together again. The Constitution of the United States makes provision for dividing the state; it makes no provision for uniting two states into one."

Trumbull then moved that action on the bill be deferred until the first Monday in December.

While the vote was being taken, Carlile and Willey engaged in a wordy battle, the latter accusing his colleague of having betrayed the people of West Virginia.

Mr. Wade came to Willey's assistance and made some illuminating statements regarding the part which Carlile had taken in framing the original bill.

"He, of all the men in the committee, is the man who penned these bills and drew them up. He is the man who has investigated all the precedents to see how far you could go in this direction. It was to his lucid mind that we were indebted for the fact that there were no legal or constitutional barriers in the way of this proposition. . . . He is the gentleman who impressed his opinions upon the committee as strongly as anybody else, and what change has come over the spirit of his dream I know not. His conversion is greater than that of St. Paul's. . . . Why did he persuade us that there was scarcely a dissenting vote in all that part of Virginia, if now he has discovered that he was wrong?"[52]

The speaker urged the passage of the bill at once, because there was no good reason why action should be deferred. Trumbull's motion to postpone was defeated; the bill was ordered to be engrossed for the third reading and was then passed by a vote of twenty-three to seventeen.

In the House, Mr. Brown stood sponsor for the West Virginia bill.

On June 25, 1862, he introduced the bill, which was read a first and a second time and referred to the Committee on Territories. The committee made its report July 16th. Upon motion of Mr. Conkling, consideration was postponed until the second Tuesday in December.

The West Virginia question possesses many interesting and surprising features. In reviewing the course of events one cannot but be struck by the fact that it was the unexpected which generally turned up.

No one would have predicted in May 1861, that John S. Carlile, the real leader in the reorganized government and the first man to propose the division of the state, would be branded as a Judas Iscariot the following year.

Likewise, no one expected to see Waitman T. Willey, known in the early part of 1861 as a pro-slavery man and thoroughly out of sympathy with the Wheeling government, take up the burden thrown off by Carlile and battle with all his might for a cause toward which he had formerly exhibited entire indifference.

### Senator Willey's Change of Heart

In the fall of 1861 Mr. Willey had openly expressed his doubt as to the constitutionality of any bill designed to form a new state in

---

[52] Willey, William P., *An Inside View of the Formation of the State of West Virginia.* (1901) p.

Virginia. His support of the project was so lukewarm that he was openly accused of working against it by the *Wheeling Intelligencer* (Oct. 14, 1861).

Carlile's most clever apologist could scarcely make out a good case for him, although he cannot be condemned solely on the ground that he changed his opinion. Much had occurred in the year following the May convention.

### West Virginia: Unwanted by West Virginians

Careful and impartial observers of the situation knew that men with strong Union principles were hard to find in any place in the state, outside of the northern panhandle – and even there, many simply sided with the Union out of a fear of what might happen had they support the Confederacy.

Enlistments in the Union army were provokingly slow and it was only through the assistance of men from Ohio and Pennsylvania that the state was able to furnish anything near her quota of troops.

All newspaper correspondents testified to the unmistakable hostility of the Western Virginians and some advised that the section be left to shift for itself.

It has been stated that in no election was there more than a small minority of votes cast. The feeling became general that this was a bad augury, Mr. M. Dent of Morgantown declared that he had been told by Colonel Evans of the 7th Virginia regiment that there were not over 1,000 Virginians in the whole Union army.

The *Wheeling Intelligencer*, on Sept. 6, 1861, printed a letter signed "Western Virginian," asserting that most of the men protecting West Virginia were from Ohio and Indiana. "Of the tens of thousands of able-bodied young and middle-aged men, how many have responded to the call?"

The Cincinnati papers were especially severe upon West Virginia, probably because they were in such close touch with the situation and saw so clearly that the people had no desire to take part in the struggle.

As time drew on and new matters presented themselves for consideration by the electorate, the apathy became dense. In special elections the returns invariably showed that the voters were deliberately staying away from the polls.

The greatest number of votes cast was in the election for state officers which occurred May 23, 1862, when 14,824 persons were reported to have taken part in the election. Mass meetings held for the purpose of nominating delegates to the various conventions were attended so poorly that in many instances they adjourned without taking any action.

Chapter
Twelve

# West Virginia
# Becomes the Thirty-Fifth Star

Congress adjourned July 17, 1862. The debates in the Senate on the West Virginia question had aroused much interest in the subject throughout the North.

### Thirty-Fifth Star: In the Media

Much like modern-day American society, the issue of West Virginia was divided along partisan lines for the press and the people – the anti-administration papers lining up solidly against the creation of a new state from Virginia.

A New York financial paper detected a disposition on the part of Congress to legislate from impulse rather than from a deep conviction founded upon close study. "If members of Congress

185

examine their own hearts, can they not detect a lurking desire to punish the Old Dominion for her infidelity by stripping her of those outlying possessions which she abandoned to neglect? . . . We would be loth to see the principle established that because the constituted authorities of a state may have acted criminally, therefore the state itself may be cut into shreds and patches."[53]

Abolition papers agreed with Senator Sumner that West Virginia was desirable only as a free state.[54]

If slavery had such an extraordinary hold upon the people that they would not consent to its abolition, then the North would be justified in rejecting their petition, especially as the legality of the procedure was questionable.

Some were unable to see any good at all that could be brought about by the admission of West Virginia, even with an abolition constitution.

As a rule, however, newspapers throughout the North were generally favorable to the West Virginia bill. Many of them had opposed the measure in 1861, but had changed their tone and now gave it hearty support.

It was the general feeling that the hands of the Federal Government should be strengthened as much as possible, and the rather vague idea prevailed that the Union cause would be aided if West Virginia was admitted.

Constitutional objections were now lost sight of in the greater question of expediency.

The *Philadelphia Press* at first warned the people of West Virginia that Congress would not recognize secession by listening to their petitions for admission.

In June 1862, however, this journal had come around to the other side and now declared that it could not see a single objection to the act of admission.

The *New York World* declared that the people of West Virginia deserved some reward for their heroic defense of the Union.

The *New York Tribune* was in favor of admission, even though the constitution of the new state was silent on the slavery question, while the *New York Post* made its support of the bill contingent upon the passage of a gradual emancipation clause.

---

[53] *The Commercial Advertiser*, July 20, 1862.
[54] *National Republican*, August 2, 1862.

The *New York* Times was inclined to be non-committal, but feared that innocent holders of Virginia bonds would suffer if the state were divided.

The *Washington Chronicle* expressed its inability to perceive any good reason why Congress should refuse admission. The whole question simply was whether Congress would recognize and protect a certain loyal community which needed its protection.

The *Cincinnati Commercial* agreed with this, and added that no attention should be paid to those who held out for immediate emancipation.

The *Utica Herald* said "The consent of the legislature of eastern Virginia has not been secured, but they are traitors and their consent may be dispensed with. The consent of the people of the east, however, is vitally necessary. Many of them are loyalists and it is not just to cut up the state while they are tied hand and foot to the rebellion."

The *New York Tribune* took upon itself the difficult task of showing why the admission of West Virginia was constitutional.

There were two rival hypotheses: first, that which regarded the insurgent states as having committed suicide by their treason and being now merely Federal territory subject to reorganization and readmission; second, that which regarded the states as still existing in the persons and acts of the loyal citizens. The Democrats in the North held the second view, but now that the administration was acting in accordance with it they changed their opinion. The West Virginia which forms the new state, said the *New York Tribune*, was totally distinct from the old Virginia that assented to it, though it happened that most of the members of the legislature were chosen from the counties which formed the new state of West Virginia.

The *National Intelligencer* took the opposite view and claimed that the act of admission would be a violation both of the United States Constitution and the state constitution. It would have to be consummated on the assumption that the secession of Virginia was an accomplished fact, so far as it regarded that portion of the state which was in rebellion against the Federal Government.

The *Wheeling Intelligencer* criticized its northern contemporaries for not familiarizing themselves with the local situation.

One half did not know that the question of separation was submitted to all the people of Virginia, and about the same proportion were under the impression that the legislature which gave its consent to the formation of the new state did not represent the whole state of Virginia.

The *Intelligencer* far overshot the mark in its zeal for the new state. For it to assert that the people of Virginia approved the division of the new state was a palpable falsehood, the chief effect of which was to mislead outside observers of the situation.

# West Virginia Statehood: Congress Votes

Tuesday, December 9, 1862, the House of Representatives took up the consideration of the Senate bill providing for the admission of West Virginia into the Union.

Representative Conway of Kansas made the first speech in opposition, urging that while West Virginia deserved all the good fortune that could come to it, its admission involved too many controversial questions of constitutionality. All depended upon the consent of the Virginia legislature, and while a liberal construction of the United States Constitution was necessary sometimes, it was not possible to stretch that document far enough to cover the case before them.

The Pierpont government, he argued, was put in operation without any legal sanction other than its recognition by the President and the Senate. This was not binding upon the House.

The Wheeling government assumed authority on the ground that the treason of the regular state officials left vacancies. These they had filled.

All this was unsatisfactory, said Conway, because a state could commit no treason and because the Pierpont clique had no right to arrogate to themselves the vacant offices.

The real importance of the situation lay in the fact that the Federal authorities might soon be called upon to take some action in eleven states whose position was like that of Virginia. A policy designed to put all the authority of a state in the hands of a few individuals calling themselves the loyal citizens of the state was a wrong one.

## Lincoln's Motivation in Creating West Virginia

We must not lose sight of the fact that far from being the iconized hero he is today, in 1862, Abraham Lincoln was an unpopular American President who was blamed for plunging the nation into a bloody civil war.

With mid-term Congressional elections on the horizon and horrifically low poll numbers, in 1862 President Abraham Lincoln's reelection to the nation's highest office was anything but an assurance.

The creation of West Virginia, argued Democrats in Congress, would consolidate all the powers of the government into the hands of the executive – and an unpopular one at that.

If the West Virginia bill passed, four Senators would be created (two from West Virginia and two from Virginia) and the President could be sure of the electoral votes of the Restored Government of Virginia as well as the newly created State of West Virginia. Thus he could build up a political machine of unparalleled strength.

### The Creation of Nevada

A year following the "disruption of Virginia," the Lincoln Administration, in October 1864, again pushed for the unorthodox creation of yet another state – Nevada.

With a hotly contested Presidential election just weeks away, Republican officials in the Federal government fast tracked Nevada's statehood in an effort to ensure the western state's electoral votes in the Presidential Election of 1864 would be counted.

In an effort to achieve statehood prior to the November 7, 1864, election, Union sympathizers in Nevada rushed to send the entire state constitution to the United States Congress by telegraph – fearing that sending it by train would not guarantee its arrival on time.

Taking two days to transmit the 16,543-word document, the proposed new state's constitution was sent to Washington on October 26—27, 1864, just two weeks prior to the election on November 7, 1864, at a cost of $4,303.27 ($64,241.89 in 2014 dollars). It was, at the time, the longest telegraph transmission ever made.

At the time of its admission into the Union, Nevada had fewer than 40,000 inhabitants – far fewer than the initial population of any other state.

Though Lincoln's fears of losing the election of 1864 proved baseless, carrying the electoral college in a landslide, his popularity throughout the North had waned considerably. In the end, he managed to secure only 55% of the popular vote.

## The Constitutional Question

When it came to the Constitutionality of Virginia, Congressman Martin F. Conway of Kansas argued that Virginia was either out of the Union and to be regarded as a foreign state, or else she was still a member of the Union and to be respected as such. The latter view now prevailed. A state could not commit treason, since treason was a crime and only individuals could commit crimes.

If the whole personnel of the state abandon its functions, it becomes United States territory subject only to Federal authority.

The regularly elected officers of Virginia had vacated their positions by virtue of their treason, but no man or set of men could legally take up these offices without being chosen according to law.

William G. Brown, one of the authors of the bill, assailed vigorously Conway's arguments. He defended the legitimacy of the Wheeling government, but touched lightly upon the constitutional principles involved.

Not only had the President and the Senate recognized the Wheeling government, but the Attorney General of the United States had made a formal decision declaring that the Wheeling authorities had lawfully assumed the power surrendered by Letcher and the other eastern Virginia officials.

The case referred to was one involving the question of the distribution from the sale of public lands. Virginia had previously refused to accept her share. The Wheeling government, being in sore need of money, applied to the Federal authorities for the $40,000 due the state. The matter was referred to Attorney General Bates, who decided that the loyal legislature of Virginia had the right to make such a request. The money was turned over to the Wheeling government."

Since the legislative powers of the people could not be annihilated, the treason of the Richmond conspirators had simply caused such powers to revert back to the people.

The Wheeling conventions were organized upon the principle that the people could assume their original rights when it became necessary to do so. The legislature which gave its consent to the division of the state was composed of the only loyal representatives of the state.

The counties included in the bill contained about 24,000 square miles and had a population of nearly 330,000. Virginia had never been a united state and never could be, because of geographical reasons. The hatred between the sections had been greatly intensified by the war. At the time the first Wheeling convention was in session Southern troops were only fifty or sixty miles away, marching with all possible speed to disperse the gathering

The proposed new state had raised sixteen regiments for the Union army, more than her quota. In his own county, said Mr. Brown, nearly every fighting man was in the army.

It was fortunate for West Virginia that its fate did not depend upon the efforts of its representatives in the House. The case was weak enough to begin with, but the crude attempts of Mr. Brown and his colleagues to justify their position would have been laughable had the Representatives really understood the situation. Opposition in the House was more determined than it had been in the Senate, in spite of the fact that the measure was free from the slavery features of the first bill.

Congressman Abram B. Olin, of New York, declared his intention of voting for the bill, but would do so mainly because the Executive Department had given the West Virginians reason to believe that their requests would meet with the approval of all departments of the government.

"But," said he, "I confess I do not fully understand upon what principles of constitutional law this measure can be justified. It cannot be done, I fear, at all. It can be justified only as a measure of policy and of necessity."

The speaker ridiculed the idea that either the spirit or the letter of the law had been complied with.

Mr. Crittenden of Kentucky was even more impressed by the constitutional obstacles in the way of the division of Virginia at that time.

All knew that Virginia was in a state of rebellion, but was still a member of the Union. When she was fully restored to her original position, her first demand would be that the sections so illegally taken from her should be given back. She would say, "I gave no consent, and there is the Constitution which says that without my consent you shall not do what you have done, and now you cannot deprive me of my rights by any such unconstitutional course of procedure."

No one really believed that the government at Wheeling was the government of Virginia. This might be inferred from the fact that the body which drew up the petition for admission was the same body which gave its consent as the Virginia legislature.

Congressman Dawes, of Massachusetts, exhibited not merely a knowledge of the legal questions involved, but also a most disconcerting familiarity with some of the points not enlarged upon by the friends of the new state.

He showed that the first Wheeling convention was deterred from taking steps toward separation from Virginia only by the suggestion of some unknown persons in Washington, that the act could better be accomplished by first setting up a reorganized government.

The Western Virginia Representatives in Congress had always claimed that the only purpose for which this convention was called was the reestablishment of the government of Virginia.

The speaker stated most emphatically that no person residing in any portion of the state but the part contemplating separation had given his consent to the act.

Two or three representatives had been "picked up" in various counties of the east, but they did not claim to represent their counties officially.

"It is trifling with the spirit of the constitution to say that any portion of the state of Virginia which is left has consented in any way, in any form and substance to the dismemberment of the state."

As for the invitation sent out to all the counties to join in the movement, it was like commanding a man bound hand and foot in prison to come forth.

Representative Stevens, of Pennsylvania, said he would vote for the bill, while knowing it to be unconstitutional.

No provision could be found to justify it on constitutional grounds.

It was mockery to say that the Virginia legislature had ever consented to the division of the state.

The body which met in Richmond was still the legislature of Virginia, although disloyal and traitorous. The state as a state was bound by its act, but not the individuals who were responsible to the general government.

"I say then that we may admit West Virginia as a new state, not by virtue of any provision of the Constitution but under our absolute power which the laws of war give us. I shall vote for this bill upon that theory and upon that alone, for I will not stultify myself by supposing that we have any warrant in the Constitution for this proceeding."

Congressman Noell, of Missouri, who also announced his intention of voting for the bill while doubting its constitutionality, asserted that they were living in revolutionary times, when they could not afford to split hairs on technical questions.

Joseph Segar, eastern Virginia's embattled representative who had been kicked out of the House for showing up with only twenty-five votes cast in his Congressional election, had by this point been accepted into the House of Representatives.

The Virginia legislator undertook to show that the bill should not be passed even if it was constitutional.

The new-state proposition did not derive its power from the people of Virginia, not even from the people of the section of the state directly concerned, he argued.

The consent of the West Virginians had never been obtained, he said. There were 55,400 people in the eleven southern counties who had never indicated their desire to join in the movement, and 27,509 citizens of three other counties had been given practically no representation at any of the Wheeling meetings.

Ten counties with a population of 50,000 did not cast a vote either on the question of dividing the state or on the new constitution.

The counties of Greenbrier, Mercer and Monroe were connected with eastern Virginia by every possible tie. It was wrong to force the people of these counties to transfer their allegiance to a government in which they had no interest and in whose formation they had no part.

The passage of the bill, finally, would turn adrift the reclaimed portions of Virginia not included in the new state and would render more difficult the reconstruction of Virginia.

Mr. Bingham, of Ohio, as the chief supporter of the bill closed the debate with a long speech in which he attempted to answer every objection that had been raised.

To the theory that West Virginia was a territory and could not be admitted because there had been no enabling act passed by Congress, he replied that such an act had not been necessary when Michigan was admitted and was not necessary now. The neglect or the refusal of a majority of the qualified voters to go to the polls had no effect upon the election. While it was undoubtedly true that the majority in any state constituted the state, yet this majority must be composed of loyal citizens. The loyal minority of Virginia were the state and had the right to administer the laws and maintain the state government. Those members of the Virginia Assembly who subscribed to the act of secession thereby disqualified themselves from serving as Senators or Representatives. Only those who took the oath to support the Constitution of the United States were ever members of any legislature of any state in the United States.

The remainder of Mr. Bingham's address was a summary of the ground already covered by previous speakers on the same side. His closing words are significant.

Referring to the emancipation policy of the President, he urged that the final recognition of the Wheeling government would give an impetus to anti-slavery:

"Declare that the legislature of the state and then upon that hypothesis admit the state; and of course once admitted its own legislative assembly will be beyond question; and when the new legislature under the new state of Virginia shall accept the President's proposition ... all doubters about the constitutionality of the act will be silent; and, whether silent or not, there will stand the record of the majority of this House to give validity to their act and from which there can be no appeal."

On December 10, 1862, the bill was passed by a strictly partisan vote of ninety-six to fifty-five.

Gideon Welles, United States Secretary of the Navy from 1861 to 1869, made the following comment in his diary: "The House has voted to create and admit Western Virginia as a state. This is not the time to divide the old Commonwealth. The requirements of the Constitution are not complied with, as they in good faith should be, by Virginia, by the proposed new state, or by the United States."

## West Virginia Statehood: Lincoln Decides

Creating a state out of Western Virginia had been long, requiring much trickery, yet against all odds the West Virginia Statehood Bill arrived at the White House in mid-December 1862 – lacking only one major hurdle: President Abraham Lincoln's signature.

Despite having sympathies for the proposed state, Lincoln realized that grave constitutional questions were involved, and that a precedent might be established which was calculated at some future time to embarrass the Government.

On December 23 he addressed a letter to the Cabinet which ran as follows:

*"A bill for an act entitled 'An Act for the Admission of the State of West Virginia into the Union and for other purposes' has passed the House of Representatives and the Senate and has been duly presented to me for my action. I respectfully ask of each of you an opinion in writing on the following questions, to-wit: First, Is the said act constitutional? Second, Is the said act expedient?"*

Six of the Cabinet members replied to Lincoln's request and their opinions were equally divided.

Seward, Chase, and Stanton answered both questions in the affirmative, while Welles, Blair, and Bates replied in the negative.

Attorney General Bates declared that the measure was both unconstitutional and inexpedient.

Congress could admit new states but could not form new states.

A free American state could be made only by its component members – the people. The state must exist as a separate independent body before admission.

In the case of West Virginia, the legislature of the whole state had not given its consent as required by the Constitution and furthermore the consent of both legislatures was necessary. No one claimed that there was any legislature of West Virginia to give its consent. The reorganized government owed its origin to necessity, not to law, and was clearly a revolutionary proceeding justified by the exigencies of the situation. It was a provisional government, whose object was not to divide but to restore the state.

Coming to the more practical side of the question, Mr. Bates asserted that the restored government never represented more than one fourth of the people of Virginia. The act of consent was less in the nature of a law than of a contract. It was a grant of power, an agreement to be divided. In the present instance the representatives of the counties included in the bill made an agreement with themselves.

"Is that fair dealing?" asked Mr. Bates. "Is that honest legislation? Is that a legitimate exercise of a constitutional power by the legislature of Virginia."

"It seems to me . . . that that is nothing less than attempted secession, hardly covered under the flimsy forms of law."

The fact that Mr. Bates was a native of Virginia may have been responsible for his feeling on the subject.

Secretary of State Seward upheld the constitutionality of the act on the ground that the United States does not recognize secession and since Virginia must be deemed as existing in the Union, the loyal portion must be the government of Virginia. "If the United States allow to that organization any of these rights, powers, and privileges it must be allowed to possess and enjoy them all. If it be a state competent to be represented in Congress and bound to pay taxes, it is a state competent to give the required consent of the state to the formation and erection of the new state of West Virginia within the jurisdiction of Virginia." The act was expedient, said Mr. Seward, first, because it would serve to give the people of West Virginia better protection, and, second, because the United States Government would derive much benefit thereby.

Mr. Chase, Secretary of the Treasury, agreed with Seward in every particular. Mr. Stanton dismissed the whole question with a few words. He could not perceive that the act was in conflict with the

Constitution of the United States, and the admission of the new state would establish a new boundary between the free and the slave states.

Mr. Welles argued that the new organization in Virginia lacked all the symbols of a state – records, traditions, capitol, etc. It did not assume any of the debts and liabilities of the old state and acted in all respects like a mere provisional government. Now it proposed to detach itself from the eastern section, something which could not be done in a regular, legal manner conformable to the letter and spirit of the Constitution. Even though the act had been constitutional it would be inexpedient at such a period of civil commotion.

Postmaster General Blair, in recording himself as opposed to the bill, stressed the point that the actual consent of the old state had never been given. Moreover, it was injurious to cut off the loyal people of Virginia in the counties not included in the Act, especially as their number far exceeded the 20,000 West Virginians who had consented to the separation.

President Lincoln read these opinions carefully before attaching his signature to the bill.

His reasons for signing the Act were given as follows:

*The consent of the legislature of Virginia is constitutionally necessary to the bill for the admission of West Virginia becoming a law. A body claiming to be such legislature has given its consent. We cannot well deny that it is such, unless we do so upon the outside knowledge that the body was chosen at elections in which a majority of the qualified voters of Virginia did not participate. But it is a universal practice . . . to give no legal consideration whatever to those who do not choose to vote, as against the effect of the votes of those who do choose to vote. Hence it is not the qualified voters, but the qualified voters who choose to vote, that constitute the political power of the state. Much less than to non-voters should any consideration be given to those who did not vote in this case, because it is also matter of outside knowledge that they were not merely neglectful of their rights under and duty to this government, but were also engaged in open rebellion against it.*

*Doubtless among these non-voters were some Union men whose voices were smothered by the more numerous Secessionists; but we know too little of their number to assign them any appreciable value. Can this government stand if it indulges constitutional constructions by which men in open rebellion against it are to be accounted, man for man, the equals of those who maintain their loyalty to it? Are they to be accounted even better citizens and more worthy of consideration than those who neglect to vote? If so, their treason against the Constitution enhances their constitutional value. Without braving these absurd conclusions, we cannot deny that the body which consents to the admission of West Virginia is the legislature of Virginia.*

*I do not think the plural form of the words 'legislatures' and 'states' in the phrase of the Constitution 'without the consent of the legislatures of the states concerned,' etc., has any reference to the new state concerned. That plural form sprang from the contemplation of two or more old states contributing to form a new one. The idea that the new state was in danger of being admitted without its own consent was not provided for because it was not thought of, as I conceive. . . .*

*But is the admission into the Union of West Virginia expedient? . . . More than on anything else, it depends on whether the admission or rejection of the new state would, under all circumstances, tend the more strongly to the restoration of the national authority throughout the Union. That which helps most in this direction is the most expedient at this time.*

*Doubtless those in remaining Virginia would return to the Union, so to speak, less reluctantly without the division of the old state than with it, but I think we could not save as much in this quarter by rejecting the new state, as we should lose by it in West Virginia. We can scarcely dispense with the aid of West Virginia in this trouble; much less can we afford to have her against us, in Congress and in the field. Her brave and good men regard her admission into the Union as a matter of life and death. They have been true to the Union under very severe trials.*

*We have so acted as to justify their hopes and we cannot fully retain their confidence and cooperation if we seem to break faith with them. In fact, they could not do so much for us, if they would. Again, the admission of the new state turns that much slave soil to free, and thus is a certain and irrevocable encroachment upon the cause of the rebellion. The division of a state is dreaded as a precedent. But a measure made expedient by a war is no precedent for times of peace. It is said that the admission of West Virginia is secession and tolerated only because it is our secession.*

*Well, if we call it by that name, there is still difference enough between secession against the Constitution and secession in favor of the Constitution. I believe the admission of West Virginia into the Union is expedient.*

After the President's signature had been attached to the West Virginia bill there yet remained one final step to be taken before a proclamation could be issued declaring the new state formally admitted into the Union.

The people must first ratify the gradual emancipation clause; and while it was a foregone conclusion that such would be done a considerable spirit of opposition developed among those who professed to fear "negro-domination."

January 14, 1863, the Schedule Commissioners recalled the constitutional convention and issued a proclamation ordering elections in five counties not heretofore represented.

In obedience to this call the convention reassembled in Wheeling February 12, 1863, with fifty-four members present representing forty-four of the forty-eight counties.

A committee known to be favorable to emancipation was appointed to consider the insertion of the necessary clause in the constitution.

February 17th an election ordinance was passed submitting the revised constitution to the people of the state. The act provided that the names of the voters should be permanently enrolled in the registration book according to their votes for or against the constitution.

March 26, 1863, the constitution as amended was ratified by a vote of 18,862 to 514; a copy was sent to President Lincoln and on April 19, 1863, he issued a proclamation declaring the admission of West Virginia completed to take effect sixty days from that time.

On June 20th, 1863, West Virginia formally took her place in the Union as the thirty-fifth state and Virginia, the mother of states and statesmen, had been dispossessed of one-third her territory.

# Chapter Thirteen

# An Illegal State of Chaos

On the afternoon of June 20, 2013, hundreds flocked to the steps of the West Virginia Capitol Building, celebrating the 150th birthday of the Mountain State.

Being a Mountaineer, my heart swells with emotion when I think about the proud and honorable history I enjoy just beyond the mountain ridges: I have a grandfather who marched atop Blair Mountain in an valiant effort to defend the weak and downtrodden, my grandmother devoted herself to the less fortunate living in her community– giving out of her own poverty, and my dad, the hardest worker I have ever known, has always stood fearless, unwavering in his devotion to the side of what is just and right. To put it simply, my family and my heritage has embodied the Western Virginia spirit for centuries. I am proud of them and I am proud of West Virginia – not the government of West Virginia, but the people of West Virginia.

Despite this proud heritage, I am also fully aware that being a West Virginian means that one is no stranger to pain and suffering.

Perhaps no words better describe the plight of the people of the Mountain State than a 1973 report issued by Governor Arch Moore's office:

*"A bridge collapses. An airplane crashes. A coal mine explodes -- and a dam fails... And people die... Such are the methods by which tragedy has, in recent years, traced a pattern of human misery and suffering in West Virginia's history."* [55]

To put it into the simplest of terms, being a West Virginian means being acquainted with struggle and sadly, much of these struggles stem from the state's illegal root. For if the root is corrupt, then one can say with a high degree of certainty that the entire fruit of such a plant will also be tarnished.

## Looking Backward & Forward

Though the majority's voice was utterly silenced throughout the dark days of America's Civil War in Western Virginia, no doubt many of the loyal Virginia southerners who returned home from the bloody and ghastly Civil War resumed their lives in the new state with an unbridled optimism regarding the future. The war was over and the future lay before them.

As was the case with my great-great-great grandfather, Thomas Benton Farley, an enlisted soldier in Logan County, Virginia's division of the 36th Virginia infantry, known locally as "the Logan Wildcats."

Captured by Union forces on September 19, 1864, in Winchester, Virginia, my grandfather was confined as a prisoner of war at the notorious Union POW camp located at Point Lookout, Maryland, where he would spend the majority of the remaining days of the conflict as a trophy of war.

Weak, hungry, penniless and defeated, Thomas B. Farley was released on March 15, 1865, and ordered to walk to his home in Logan County, now West Virginia, more than 300 miles to the west.

---

[55] The Buffalo Creek Flood and Disaster: Official Report from the Governor's Ad Hoc Commission of Inquiry (1973)

Undoubtedly the +1.5 million-foot journey provided incredible opportunities for thinking for my ancestor: Thinking of the past and the ravages of war he had witnessed and to which he had been a party.

Thinking of the present – of General Robert E. Lee's surrender at Appomattox, President Lincoln being murdered in Washington and news of his own president, Jefferson Davis, dishonorably fleeing the South as Northern retribution swiftly flooded into Dixie.

Still yet, I simply cannot help but imagine that his mind was also fixated upon the future.

No longer was he a Virginian, no longer was he a soldier, no longer was he a rebel, no longer was the land of the free tarnished by the vile and disgusting practice of human slavery. He was an American and he was now a West Virginian.

In the years ahead, Farley would be elected by his fellow citizens to serve as justice of the peace and assessor of Logan County.

He would also become an early leader in the newly created locality of Mingo County.

The man who was born in 1837 lived to see incredible changes in the land upon which "God shed His grace."

Born in an era when Texas was a sovereign independent nation, decades before the Pony Express was ever incorporated, he died in a nation that had fought a world war using aircraft.

Though he never moved more than a mile from his original starting place – the old shack in which he was born – everything around him had changed by the time of his death in 1922.

The community of Burch, Logan County, Virginia, the place of his birth, had been transformed into the Town of Delbarton, Mingo County, West Virginia, at the time of his death.

From relatives I have spoken with and evidences found in the old family Bible, it is apparent that like so many other mountaineers who went off to fight for their native Virginia, only to return and find themselves no longer Virginians, my great-great-great grandfather spent the remainder of his days with one eye looking forward and the other eye looking backwards – back to a time when West Virginia was Western Virginia and back to a day when mountaineers truly were free.

We know he looked forward because he raised a house full of "young'ns," fifteen to be exact, but we also know that he never ceased to remember that despite what the map said, he was a Virginian.

On November 2, 1884, he named his son Thomas Jefferson Farley, no doubt after one of Virginia's most famous residents and champion of state's rights.

Four years later, in December 1888, my grandfather named a daughter Dixie Farley.

Twenty-three years after departing from the Maryland POW camp, the memory of Dixie was so alive for my grandfather that he chose to bestow it upon his daughter.

Southern West Virginia, like all of Dixie, never forgot the time their young men drew a hard line in the sand and stood in defense of their native state and he stood in defense of the Commonwealth of Virginia.

Unlike the rest of Dixie, however, the boys from southern West Virginia paid the heaviest toll. In their quest to defend their state, they lost the identity of their very homes.

Still, these men never lost sight of the fact that they were Virginians and they never forgot the hellish years they spent in battle for the Old Virginny.

The photograph below (Photo credit: Harlan Justice) features the men of my great-great-great grandfather's Confederate Army division, the "Logan Wildcats."

Taken at a reunion in 1900 in Chapmanville, the grainy image reveals a group of feeble men with canes and long beards, but more than that, it reminds us that not all West Virginians were West Virginians by choice, in fact, most of the abled bodied men from the state's southern counties became West Virginians at gunpoint and only after years of killing and being killed.

The sons of Logan, McDowell, Greenbrier and dozens of other counties fought the Civil War for the same reason most others their age went to war for the South – because their state requested their service.

They did not own slaves and most couldn't have cared less – they were mere pawns in an old rich man's game of war. Sadly, for the inhabitants of this region, the game has yet to end.

# A State that got Bought

In the years following my grandfather's return to Logan County and as the smoke began to clear from the Civil War, the nation entered into the industrial revolution and the limitless resources of West Virginia's coal and timber seemed irresistible to many of the country's wealthiest companies.

Without the protection of an established government in Richmond, slick-tongued lawyers and wealthy tycoons descended upon the illegal state, finding refuge in none other than the newly created state's corrupt government.

The late Matewan resident, Joseph P. Garland, stated that his grandfather, who was illiterate, was tricked into giving up 1,666 acres of the family's land for a single shotgun.

"They've [southern West Virginians] been robbed, raped and cheated out of their land," stated Garland.

Despite the state's incredible wealth, few natives were ever able to enjoy much gain from the rich resources abounding in the area, as outside corporations quickly gobbled up much of the territory of southern West Virginia.

Aided by the natural transportation route provided by the Tug River, outside loggers moved into the area and cleared many of the region's most valuable woodland.

The arrival of the N&W Railroad allowed for the timber to be shipped east, further accelerating the rate of the state's deforestation.

At the turn of the century, non-residents owned over half the land in Mingo County, West Virginia, as was the case in several other coalfield counties.

Observing this problem, William MacCorkle, West Virginia Governor, warned the state legislature in his inaugural address on March 4, 1893, that "the state is rapidly passing under the control of large foreign and non-resident landowners." He cautioned that "the men who are today purchasing the immense acres of the most valuable lands in the state are not citizens and have only purchased in order that they may carry to their distant homes in the North the usufruct of the lands of West Virginia."

MacCorkle, the son of a Confederate Major and sixth consecutive Democratic governor of West Virginia (*the fact that West Virginia had a Democratic governor for 26 consecutive years following the 1860s should lend credence to the fact that the State's residents were unabashedly southern in their loyalties*) witnessed his dire warning prove true.

Within seven years' time, destructive logging techniques had removed half of the state's forests. Nearly all of the state's timber resources had been exhausted within two decades.

For the first time in its history, West Virginia was viewed as an eyesore. One visiting writer described the state as "a monotonous panorama of destruction."

Ronald Eller, a professor of history at the University of Kentucky describes the effects of 'absentee landownership' in the following way:

*Because of absentee ownership of the state's resources, the dollars that could have built better schools and better roads and better health services in the early part of the century flowed out of the region and we got what we call 'growth without development.' We got a short period of immense growth and expansion and boom period and jobs, but we didn't get the development of those aspects that will sustain a community over time and provide a quality of life.* [56]

---

[56] West Virginia: A Film History, West Virginia Humanities Council.

# A People are Enslaved

Perhaps the most heartbreaking element regarding the creation of the State of West Virginia is this – While the rest of the nation was casting off the evil chains of slavery in the closing days of the nineteenth century, the groundwork was being laid in the Appalachian Mountains of West Virginia for a new people to be enchained.

In the century ahead, the plantations and cotton fields of Georgia gave way to the mines and company towns of Matewan and Paint Creek.

The slave owners were replaced with distant industrial corporations profiteering on the backs of America's once independent mountaineers. And taskmasters were exchanged for notorious mercenaries and terrorists such as the Baldwin-Felts Detectives, whose acts of brutality are unrivaled by even the most demonic slave owners.

It is both heartbreaking and frightening to witness how quickly the mountain people of southern West Virginia went from being known as the free spirited Scotch-Irish to impoverished miners living in coal camps begging for just a temporary respite.

### A Painful Occupation is Born:

The industrial revolution created a demand for coal that had outpaced supply, causing the price of the mineral to skyrocket more than four-fold.

For the first time in history, it had actually become profitable to extract the coal buried beneath the hills of southern West Virginia.

With the price of coal now quadrupled, mining companies rushed into the Appalachian Mountains of Southern West Virginia and quickly created railroads linking the region to the outside world.

The rising number of factories popping up across the nation in the opening days of the 1900s created an endless demand for coal.

By 1918, the industry was experiencing record sales, totaling 579 million tons of bituminous coal.

Aided by railroads which tore through the countryside, coal companies soon found themselves reaching a level of power that had previously been thought unattainable.

Owning countless square miles of land, coal companies created company towns, where miners and their families lived, worked and worshipped – under the watchful eye of mine bosses.

Crandall Shiflett, author of the 1991 publication, *Coal Towns Life, Work, and Culture in Company Towns of Southern Appalachia 1880-1960*, described these company-owned communities in the following way:

*Usually, the coal camp, like the railroad camp, began with temporary housing-tents or boardinghouses – until more permanent dwellings could be built. Gradually, within a year or so, the camp grew into a company store, the most essential structure in the town...*

As mining operations in company towns grew, coal companies would introduce other buildings, including schools and churches.

Ever increasing their power and control, mining companies soon began paying workers with scrip, a private currency issued by mining companies to their employees.

The argument for paying their workers in scrip was that the secluded location of mining communities made it difficult to provide cash to the miners; however, a 1911 report by the Immigration Commission found that in some cases, miners were receiving only 30% of their wages in cash.

According to Lou Athey, the Charles A. Dana professor emeritus of history at Franklin & Marshall College in Pennsylvania,

*Coal companies received significant advantages in using scrip. Scrip reduced the outflow of capital, strengthened company cash flow, and reduced payroll theft, thereby lowering the cost of security... Miners often received pay envelopes marked with a curling line across them, a symbol miners called the 'bobtail check' or the 'snake.' It meant no wages due.* [57]

Though coal companies refused to exchange scrip with legal tender, some miners found other locals willing to purchase coal scrip for a fraction of its value.

---

[57] Athey, Lou "Scrip." e-WV: The West Virginia Encyclopedia. 29 October 2010. Web. 28 October 2015.

To combat this, a 1925 West Virginia law, driven by coal lobbyists who controlled the illegal state's government, made it unlawful for scrip to be transferred to a third party. This law further solidified the company's power over employees, effectively holding them hostage from escaping to other jobs or regions of the nation.

Within a generation, an entire workforce stood at the mercy of coal companies dedicated to pillaging the land for all it was worth.

### A People Rise Up:

Realizing the difficulty that would accompany any attempts at unionizing the state's non-union southern counties, union boss John L. Lewis sent the famed labor organizer Mary Harris Jones, commonly known as Mother Jones, to rally the miners into striking.

Jones, a native of Ireland, worked previously as a teacher and dressmaker, until her husband and four children all died of yellow fever and her workshop was destroyed in a fire.

In her first trip to the Mountain State, Jones successfully convinced workers to strike and was subsequently tried for "ignoring an injunction banning meetings by striking miners," one of many times the laws of the Mountain State have violated the basic human rights guaranteed by the United States Constitution.

During her 1902 trial, a West Virginia district attorney denounced her to the court, "There sits the most dangerous woman in America... She comes into a state where peace and prosperity reign... crooks her finger [and] twenty thousand contented men lay down their tools and walk out."

Jones' fame grew rapidly after a strike turned bloody during the Paint Creek-Cabin Creek strike in 1912, when striking Kanawha County miners found themselves at the abuse of Baldwin-Felts detectives, a notorious group which specialized in breaking up unions, with the protection of law enforcement.

The Kanawha County strike has been estimated to have cost $100,000,000 and is believed to be directly responsible for at least fifty violent deaths, and many more indirectly, through starvation and malnutrition.

Following the strike, Jones was placed under house arrest in central West Virginia, until she smuggled out a message through a trapdoor to Indiana's pro-labor senator.

She was released after a total of 85 days of imprisonment.

Mother Jones arrived in Mingo County in 1920 and successfully persuaded approximately 3,000 Mingo and Logan county miners to defy company orders and enlist in the union.

Signing their union cards at the Matewan Community Church, the miners returned to work and awaited what would become swift retribution.

Quick to act, the Stone Mountain Coal Corporation fought back with mass firings, harassment, and evictions.

In an effort to retain southern West Virginia's non-union status, the company called in the notorious Baldwin-Felts detectives to assist in intimidating the miners and carrying out evictions upon the homes of workers who had been blacklisted for joining the union.

On the rainy morning of May 19, 1920, thirteen Baldwin-Felts detectives stopped off the No. 29 morning train in Matewan, carrying briefcases containing submachine guns.

According to second-hand accounts, the detectives were greeted by the town's police chief and deputy, who asked the men what they were doing in Matewan.

"We've come down here on a job. The coal company has asked us to put those people out of the houses and that is what our intentions are... We're strictly goin' to do that," replied Albert Felts.

Police Chief Sid Hatfield then warned the men that doing so would, "lead to trouble," to which Felts replied, "well, we're prepared..."

By the day's end, seven Baldwin-Felts Detectives, two miners and the community's beloved mayor lay dead in the dusty streets of Matewan.

As they have often done throughout their history, the people of West Virginia rose up to defend freedom in its hour of maximum danger.

1921 would prove to be one of the deadliest years in West Virginia's history, as West Virginia's citizens, tired of being abused for years by their own state's government, rose up against the institution in late-August.

Marching from the state's capitol building into Southern West Virginia, the miners assembled in the largest labor uprising in United States history and what was the largest armed uprising since the Civil War.

Over the next week, roughly 10,000 out gunned West Virginia coal miners bravely took on 3,000 lawmen and security officials working for coal mines, demanding their basic constitutional rights which had been denied by the new state's government.

Known today as the Battle of Blair Mountain, over one-million rounds are estimated to have been fired during the Logan County battle, which ultimately left nearly 130 individuals dead.

The September 3, 1921, edition of *The Huntington Herald* quotes one of the warring miners as having said, "We're not fighting Uncle Sam... Many of us fought in the army overseas. I did myself, but this isn't what we fought for..."

In the end, nearly 1,000 miners were indicted for murder, conspiracy to commit murder, accessory to murder, and treason against the State of West Virginia.

It would not be for another generation until miners in Southern West Virginia would earn the basic right to unionize – a right denied to them by their own state government.

## Moving Forward

There is a saying that is often whispered in the halls of West Virginia government buildings, "Thank God for Mississippi."

West Virginia is routinely at the bottom of all lists pertaining to anything good and near the top of lists pertaining to anything bad.

In Chapter One of this book, we touched on the "Tale of Two Virginias," briefly comparing Old Virginia with West Virginia.

Today, the Commonwealth of Virginia's unemployment rate ranks among one of the lowest in the nation, while that posted by the State of West Virginia qualifies as the nation's highest.

When it comes to per capita incomes, Virginia is ranked seventh in the nation, while West Virginia places 49th out of 50 states.

Most sadly, however, is the Center for Disease Control and Prevention statistic which states that a person living in West Virginia can expect to live approximately four fewer years than someone across the mountain in Virginia.

These are real and undeniable statistics.

There will be some who will argue that comparing Virginia and West Virginia is unfair – Virginia has ocean front, naval bases, borders the nation's capital.

All of this is true, however, it is important to remember that had the hasty and illegal creation of West Virginia never occurred, all of these resources would today be available to the people just over the mountain – many of which are geographically closer to these places than the average Virginia resident.

But what can we do to improve the quality of life for West Virginia in today's modern-era? Sure, we can complain about what should have been, what could have been and what shouldn't have been, but at the end of the day, the people of West Virginia, particularly southern West Virginia, need forward-looking solutions.

In January 2011, a freshman delegate from Berkeley County, Larry Kump, proposed a bill to the state legislature that would allow certain counties an opportunity to be returned to Virginia, should the voters so choose.

Speaking to the media[58], Kump stated, "I take pride in being a Mountaineer... [But] our per capita income in West Virginia is 47th in the United States; it's one of the few things we're not 50th in... We've lost 10,000 manufacturing jobs over the past three years. Gross Domestic Product is 49th in the nation... I'd prefer West Virginians stay together and just get their act together—but if they don't, I think it's a good idea to go elsewhere."

Though one can't help but admire the lawmaker's bold idea, at this point, West Virginia simply is.

It is the reality.

It is the state I describe as home.

And it is our effort to make her everything she should be – even if her birth was illegitimate.

"So then why are you writing this book," asked my mother, unsure of why I would plead the case that West Virginia was formed illegally but refuse to demand she be returned to the Old Dominion.

My answer is simple – Because we as a people must recognize that when the laws of the land are not followed, specifically the United States Constitution, we will often reap corruption, heartache and difficulty.

---

[58] "West Virginia Legislator Hatches Plan to Secede," Mother Jones, February 1, 2011.

The people of West Virginia have been paying for the sins of a handful of men for over a century and a half and little to no relief is appearing on the horizon.

To quote Ronald Reagan, "Freedom is never more than one generation away from extinction. We didn't pass it to our children in the bloodstream. It must be fought for, protected, and handed on for them to do the same."

*What can we do to right the course?*
Diversify:
Any community built around a single industry, albeit coal, a large manufacturer, tourism or anything else, is just one phone call away from looking like a ghost town along historic US-66... or US-52 for that matter.

The reality is that for better or worse, coal is a dying form of energy and is quickly being overtaken by natural gas as well as alternative fuels. Personally, this is a hard pill for me to swallow, as my family has been employed for generations by the industry and I was educated on money my dad brought home from the coal mines. I am and have always been a friend of sensible and responsible coal mining.

Unfortunately, the writing is on the wall and the longer we sit around complaining about it versus looking for new industries to fill these voids, the farther we are going to be behind when the inevitable finally happens. We must act and we must act quickly. We must remove the barriers that presently view job creators as enemy of the state and recognize that a code book written to guard against the enemies of a century ago is archaic and in desperate need of changing.

Remove Reckless Government:
It was reckless government that created West Virginia and it was an unchecked government that allowed its own people to be abused by outside corporations throughout the first half of the 1900s.

The only solution to making West Virginia the "Best Virginia" she can possibly be, however, will be in the people of the state actually stepping up to the occasion and boldly determining to reign in their own government.

Since its creation, "do gooders" from outside the region have always viewed West Virginians as nothing more than the poor and helpless folks of "App-ah-lay-sha," because after all, they are far too uneducated to find a way out on their own.

Big Brother Government arrived on the scene back in the 1960s and has been doling out clothing vouchers, food stamps and countless other "entitlements" to virtually anyone who desires to sign on the dotted line ever since.

Don't get me wrong, I fully understand that people fall upon hard times and that in a civilized society a safety net is necessary, unfortunately, what I see on a daily basis in my travels throughout the Mountain State is not a safety net of human—aid, but a hammock of government handouts.

Over my lifetime, I have watched the destruction of my community and the one person to be blamed above all others is the government. It was Uncle Sam's "war on poverty" that has been the biggest culprit in seeing poverty flourish for generations.

While many in West Virginia work +70 hours each week, barely hoping to "get by" and satisfied with what they get, their neighbors and countless others around them have inherited a mentality of "Why work when I can get my meals, housing, electricity, healthcare, clothing and anything else I want — including pills — from the government... free of charge?"

To use a term I often heard my dear ole mother say, "Why buy the cow when you can get the milk for free?"

A true story – I was recently in a tiny grocery store in McDowell County, West Virginia, and went to purchase my milk at the counter. The cashier, noticing the crinkled five dollar bill in my hand, looked at me with a face of absolute astonishment.

"Are you not paying with food stamps," she asked, bewildered by the fact any person would even think about buying milk with cash.

Uncle Sam's free goodie bag of stuff has in turn removed the incentives for the common people to diversify their local economies from the coal industry.

The excess time so many now have on their hands, has resulted in generations "looking for a buzz" when they should be looking for a job and has culminated in a government funded prescription drug addiction that is destroying lives, families and the state itself.

West Virginia has the nation's highest rate of drug overdose deaths.

Things have become so bad that the *West Virginia Executive* referred to the state's addiction as "An Economic Burden,"[59] stating, "...while the physical and mental aspects have been devastating, prescription drugs are costing more than lives..."

The economic burden brought on by the state's drug addiction totals to nearly $1 billion annually.

Return to Values:

Though it may sound trite, there is nothing wrong with West Virginia that cannot be cured by what is right with West Virginia... and what is right with West Virginia is her people – a proud and industrious people willing to pay any price necessary to provide the best life possible for their children.

This entire book may come across to some as offensive and mean-spirited to the Mountain State, this, however, is the farthest thing from my intention or the truth.

This manuscript has been penned with a sacred love for West Virginia from someone who has lived in West Virginia on and off throughout his entire life and has faced the common problems pressing the state on a daily basis.

Until we properly understand our history, recognizing the course that has brought us to this point, properly perceive things as they are and not as we desire them to be, and commit ourselves to facing difficult decisions head on, we will not prevail and things in my favorite state will only digress.

West Virginia is worth fighting for and so are our children.

---

[59] "The Cost of Addiction: An Economic Burden for West Virginia," West Virginia Executive, February 25, 2015

*Abraham Lincoln Walks at Midnight* Statue on the grounds of the West Virginia State Capitol. Photo credit: "Snoopywv"

# Those West Virginia Hills

*Oh, the West Virginia hills! How majestic and how grand,*
*With their summits bathed in glory, Like our Prince Immanuel's Land!*
*Is it any wonder then, That my heart with rapture thrills,*
*As I stand once more with loved ones On those West Virginia hills?*

*Oh, the West Virginia hills! Where my childhood hours were passed,*
*Where I often wandered lonely, And the future tried to cast;*
*Many are our visions bright, Which the future ne'er fulfills;*
*But how sunny were my daydreams On those West Virginia hills!*

*Oh, the West Virginia hills! How unchang'd they seem to stand,*
*With their summits pointed skyward To the Great Almighty's Land!*
*Many changes I can see, Which my heart with sadness fills;*
*But no changes can be noticed In those West Virginia hills.*

*Oh, the West Virginia hills! I must bid you now adieu.*
*In my home beyond the mountains I shall ever dream of you;*
*In the evening time of life, If my Father only wills,*
*I shall still behold the vision Of those West Virginia hills.*

*Oh, the hills, beautiful hills, How I love those West Virginia hills!*
*If o'er sea o'er land I roam, Still I'll think of happy home,*
*And my friends among the West Virginia hills.*

# Other Books By the Author

### The Ghosts of Mingo County

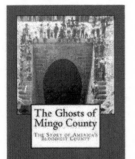

Beginning with the county's formation, as a result of an illegal liquor still, Jeremy T.K. Farley sets out telling Bloody Mingo's story; including events such as the Mingo Mine Wars, Matewan Massacre, murder of Sid Hatfield, Dingess Tunnel, Kermit Mine Explosion of 1951, Marshall University Plane Crash, community of Vulcan's application for Soviet Aid, Kermit arrests of 1986, Sheriff Eugene Crum's assassination and so much more! In this book, you will find that the story of Mingo County isn't always a pretty story. Neither is it a story the average reader is capable of stomaching, but it is a true story and it is a story worthy of being told. A true story of a place whose halls of history are littered with dead bodies, marred by greed and haunted by ghosts that just won't die.

★★★★☆
4.7 out of 5 stars

### The Civil War Out My Window

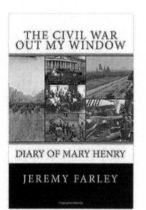

The daughter of Joseph Henry, one of America's most renowned scientists, Mary Henry was 21-years-old when her family moved into the only castle in Washington, D.C., the Smithsonian Institution Building. A prolific writer and astute observer, Mary began recording a diary in 1858, including a daily log of her personal reflections, events at the Smithsonian and conversations she had shared with many of the most influential leaders in America. It would have been impossible for the youthful lady, filled with juvenile yearnings and wanderlust, to have imagined the unspeakable horrors that would soon fill the pages of her blank diary, as she penned her first entry in November 1858. Mary's entries include personal conversations with Abraham Lincoln, General Ulysses S. Grant, common citizens and captured southern troops. A staunch unionist and American patriot, the young woman's diary reveals the incredible dilemma held by millions of Americans throughout the war between the states – as she often sympathized with the southern

★★★★★
5.0 out of 5 stars

plight, mourned Confederate causalities and criticized the Lincoln administration's every move. Though her writings provide one of the greatest insights into the Civil War in the past quarter-century, Mary's diary is far more than a collection of random thoughts on matters of science and politics. Her diary is a story of both a young woman and a struggling nation coming to age in the latter half of the nineteenth century.

54159756R00133

Made in the USA
Lexington, KY
03 August 2016